A Year in Picture Books

A Year in Picture Books

Linking to the Information Literacy Standards

Patricia A. Messner and Brenda S. Copeland

LIBRARIES
UNLIMITED
A Member of the Greenwood Publishing Group

Westport, Connecticut • London

Library of Congress Cataloging-in-Publication Data

Messner, Patricia A.
  A year in picture books : linking to the information literacy standards / Patricia A. Messner
and Brenda S. Copeland.
    p. cm.
  Includes bibliographical references and index.
  ISBN-13: 978–1–59158–495–7 (alk. paper)
  1. Library orientation for school children—United States. 2. Information literacy—Study and
teaching (Primary)—Activity programs. 3. Elementary school libraries—Activity programs—
United States. 4. Picture books for children—Educational aspects—United States. I. Copeland,
Brenda S. II. Title.
  Z711.25.S36M47 2007
  025.5678—dc22   2007013613

British Library Cataloguing in Publication Data is available.

Library of Congress Catalog Card Number: 2007013613
ISBN-13: 978–1–59158–495–7

First published in 2007

Libraries Unlimited, 88 Post Road West, Westport, CT 06881
A Member of the Greenwood Publishing Group, Inc.
www.lu.com

Printed in the United States of America

∞™

The paper used in this book complies with the
Permanent Paper Standard issued by the National
Information Standards Organization (Z39.48–1984).

10 9 8 7 6 5 4 3 2 1

Dedicated to our husbands, Bill and Joel, who have followed us to conferences and book signings. Thanks for keeping our accounts in order.

Contents

Part Four
December

Kindergarten

First Grade

Second Grade

Third Grade

Part Five
January

Kindergarten

First Grade

Second Grade

Third Grade

Part Six
February

Kindergarten

First Grade

Second Grade

Third Grade

Part Seven
March

Part Eight
April

Part Nine
May

Foreword

The library media center is under the microscope these days as more and more schools are becoming aware of the importance of a strong library program. In this project, we have chosen picture books to reinforce the AASL/AECT Information Literacy Standards for Student Learning and have zeroed in on many of the library skills that need to be taught at the elementary level. The Information Literacy Standards for Student Learning can be found at www.ala.org or in *Information Power: Building Partnerships for Learning* by the American Association of School Librarians and Association for Educational Communications and Technology.

This selection of lessons is designed for grades kindergarten through third grade and follow the school year, September through May. Our nine units serve as a guide to help the librarian align the library curriculum with the Information Literacy Standards. The themes for each of these months are as follows:

September	Orientation to the Library
October	Arrangement of the Library
November	Reading Enrichment
December	Understanding Information
January	Gathering Information
February	Using Information
March	Online Catalog
April	Information on the Internet
May	Information on the Internet

The lessons are written for a thirty-minute class time and provide objectives, skills, materials, worksheets, and pages for overhead transparencies. When using overhead transparencies copied from printed materials, remember the fair-use issue. Educators may use overheads for a year, but after the year is up they will need to make new ones.

We have studied the guidelines for both the Ohio and Pennsylvania benchmarks and feel this collection of lesson plans is just the beginning in teaching those standards. As fellow librarians, we hope these ideas get the creative juices flowing and that you will find lots of ways to use picture books to strengthen your elementary library curriculum. Strong library programs are the key to success in school. The idea that "librarians only check out books" is antiquated. To keep pace with the changes in the educational process and the "No Child Left Behind" initiative, we need to step up and take an active part in the education of all students.

Information Literacy Standards for Student Learning

American Association of School Libraries (AASL) and
Association for Educational Communication and Technology (AECT), 1998.

Information Literacy

Standard 1: The student who is information literate accesses information efficiently and effectively.

Standard 2: The student who is information literate evaluates information critically and competently.

Standard 3: The student who is information literate uses information accurately and creatively.

Independent Learning

Standard 4: The student who is an independent learner is information literate and pursues information related to personal interests.

Standard 5: The student who is an independent learner is information literate and appreciates literature and other creative expressions of information.

Standard 6: The student who is an independent learner is information literate and strives for excellence in information seeking and knowledge generation.

Social Responsibility

Standard 7: The student who contributes positively to the learning community and to society is information literate and recognizes the importance of information to a democratic society.

Standard 8: The student who contributes positively to the learning community and to society is information literate and practices ethical behavior in regard to information and information technology.

Standard 9: The student who contributes positively to the learning community and to society is information literate and participates effectively in groups to pursue and generate information.

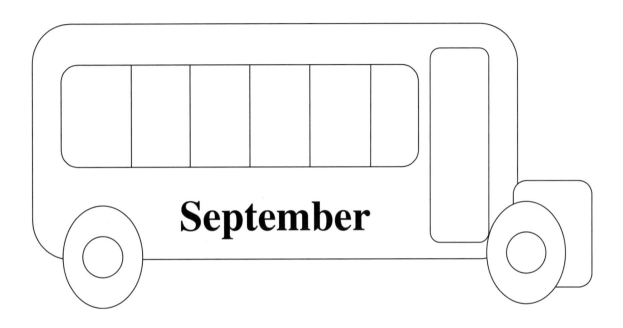

September

Curious George Visits the Library

By Margaret and H.A. Rey

Rey, Margaret, and H. A. Rey. *Curious George Visits the Library*. Boston: Houghton Mifflin, 2003.

Objective: Students will listen to the story and pick out the places in the library that Curious George visits and then take a tour of the library.

AASL Standard

Information Literacy

Standard 1: The student who is information literate accesses information efficiently and effectively.

Skills

- Library awareness

Grade Level: Kindergarten

Materials

- Yellow construction paper
- Copy of the hat pattern
- Copy of the scavenger hunt clues
- Dry eraser board and marker

Preparing the materials: Copy and cut the clues into individual cards. Add clues to personalize the clues to your individual library. Cut out eight yellow hats (see pattern), glue the clues onto the hats, and laminate. Hide the hats with clues 2–8 so that the students can find locations in your library. Examples include the following: Nonfiction, Everybody, or Easy sections; shelf markers; magazine section; tables; story corner; and circulation desk. Each individual library will have different names for these locations and will need to be modified. Clue number 1 will be the clue you begin with when touring the library.

Step 1: Introduce the book by asking if they have heard about this curious monkey. Give time for sharing. Ask the students to listen for all of the things that Curious George sees in the library.

Step 2: Read the story and share the pictures.

Step 3: Make a list on the board of things that Curious George saw in the library.

Step 4: Explain that Curious George came to our library earlier and hid some yellow hats. Using clue number 1, lead the students in a tour of the library to find the hats. As you guide them through the clues, you may wish to stop and talk about each clue. Example: This is a good time to model how the shelf markers hold the place on the shelf while the students check to see if this is the book they wish to check out.

Closure: Help students select books to take home.

1. **Books about real things.**	2. **Books about pretend things and easy to read.**
3.	4.
5.	6.
7.	8.

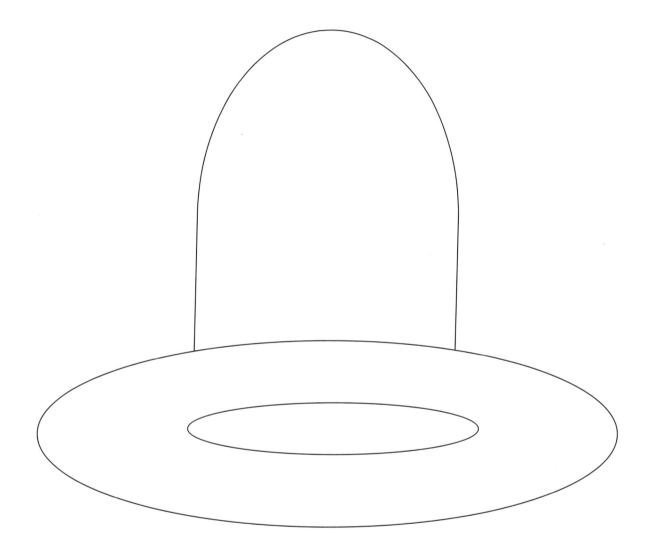

Mr. Wiggle's Book

By Paula Craig and Carol Thompson

Craig, Paula, and Carol Thompson. *Mr. Wiggle's Book.* Columbus, OH: Waterbird Books, 2004.

Objective: Students will listen to the story and identify how to care for books correctly and incorrectly.

AASL Standard

Information Literacy

Standard 1: The student who is information literate accesses information efficiently and effectively.

Skills

• Proper book care

Grade Level: First grade

Materials

• Backpack	• Eyeglasses
• Markers	• Scissors
• Crayons	• Bookmark
• Can of soda pop	• Pattern for word cards
• Bar of soap	• Card stock
• Pencil	• Chalkboard or dry eraser board
• Candy bar wrapper	• Copy of promise
• Kleenex	• Pencils
• Flashlight	

Preparing the materials: Collect items on the materials list and place them in the backpack. Copy word cards onto cardstock, cut apart, and laminate. Copy enough cards for each student to have two cards, good and bad. Prepare a copy of the promise for each student.

Step 1: Introduce the book, author, and illustrator. Tell the students they will need to listen for ways they should not treat or handle library books.

Step 2: Read the book and share the pictures.

Step 3: Students will recall things that happened to Mr. Wiggle's book in the story.

Record students' responses on the chalkboard or dry eraser board.

Step 4: Pass out word cards.

Step 5: Using the full backpack, draw out the items one at a time and have students show the correct word card that tells what kind of a friend the item is to a book. Example: "Markers" would be a bad friend to a book.

Step 6: After all items have been revealed, have students sort items into two piles, good and bad.

Closure: Have students promise to take care of books by signing a promise slip (see pattern).

Good	Bad
Good	Bad
Good	Bad
Good	Bad
Good	Bad

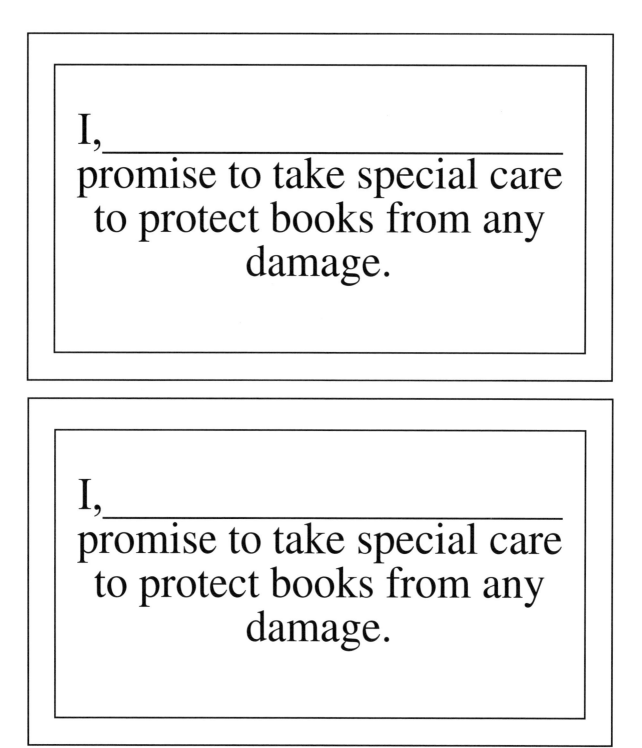

I,_____
promise to take special care
to protect books from any
damage.

I,_____
promise to take special care
to protect books from any
damage.

I.Q. Goes to the Library

By Mary Ann Fraser

Fraser, Mary Ann. *I.Q. Goes to the Library.* New York: Walker & Company, 2003.

Objective: Students will listen to the story, recall areas of the library that I.Q. explored, and compare the students' library to I.Q.'s library.

AASL Standard

Information Literacy

Standard 1: The student who is information literate accesses information efficiently and effectively.

Skills

- Library awareness

Grade Level: Second grade

Materials

- Worksheet copied for each student
- Pencils
- Clip boards for each student

Step 1: Introduce author and title. Tell students they need to listen for all the areas of the library that I.Q. explored during library week.

Step 2: Read the story and share the pictures.

Step 3: Pass out worksheets, pencils and clip boards.

Step 4: Complete the left hand side of the worksheet together as a class.

Step 5: Direct students to walk around the library and record the areas of their library on the right-hand side of the worksheet.

Step 6: Gather students and share worksheets.

Closure: Students check out books to take home.

Teacher's Notes:

I.Q.'s library has	My library has
1._____	1._____
2._____	2._____
3._____	3._____
4._____	4._____
5._____	5._____
6._____	6._____

My favorite part of my library is_____
_____.
I like this part of the library because_____
_____.

That's Our Librarian!

By Ann Morris

Morris, Ann. *That's Our Librarian!* Brookfield, CT: Millbrook Press, 2003.

Objective: Students will listen to the story and compare and contrast the job of a librarian with a student's career choice.

AASL Standards

Information Literacy

Standard 3: The student who is information literate uses information accurately and creatively.

Independent Learning

Standard 4: The student who is an independent learner is information literate and pursues information related to personal interests.

Skills

- Library awareness

- Research

- Compare and contrast

Grade Level: Second grade

Materials

- Copy of the worksheet

- Make the worksheet into an overhead

- Collection of nonfiction books about different careers (examples: *A Day with a Mechanic* by Joanne Winne or *We Need Principals* by Jane Scoggins Bauld)

- Personal pictures of your family, home, activities, and career

Preparing the materials: Display your pictures in an interesting fashion and label. Make them simple and easy to read. Example: This is my pet dog Muffy. A notebook format with plastic sleeves for the picture pages that you create works well for this project.

Step 1: Before reading this book, point out that this is a fact book, or nonfiction story. It has real photos of a librarian in New York City. Read the story and share the pictures.

Step 2: Pass out worksheets and, with help from the students, make a list on the overhead of the things that the librarian from the story did each day while the students record answers on their worksheet. Keep them simple so that slower students can keep up with the copying process.

Step 3: Review the list and explain to the students that they will research another career and record facts on the other half of their worksheet. Share the book titles that you have collected.

Step 4: Divide the students up according to the students' personal career choice. (Select books that are picture-friendly because at this age they need pictures as well as written materials.)

Closure: Return to the larger group and share facts. Vote on the career that is the most interesting.

Optional Idea: Share the pictures of your personal life. If possible include a picture of when you were in school at about the age of your students. Students will enjoy reading and looking at your display or photo notebook, so leave this out for free-time browsing.

Teacher's Notes:

I love books!

Librarian

My career

Wild about Books

By Judy Sierra

Sierra, Judy. *Wild about Books.* New York: Alfred A. Knopf, 2004.

Objective: Students will listen to the story and find book titles for the different genres in the library.

AASL Standard

Information Literacy

Standard 1: The student who is information literate accesses information efficiently and effectively.

Skills

- Library awareness

Grade Level: Third grade

Materials

- Labels for nonfiction, magazines, fiction, easy or everybody, reference, and biographies. You can print your own or use any number that are available on the market today

- Copy of the worksheet and pencils for each group

- White marker board and marker

- Several kinds of stuffed animals that could be found in a zoo

Preparing the materials: Label the main book sections in your library. Most librarians do this at the start of each year to help kids with word recognition and book location. If you have already done this part of the lesson, you are ahead of the game.

Step 1: Introduce the book by sharing the title and author. Ask students to listen for all the different kinds of books that are mentioned in the story that the animals read at the zoo.

Step 2: Read the story and share the pictures.

Step 3: With the help of the students, make a list of the books on the board that were mentioned in the reading. Take turns sending a student with the correct stuffed animal to locate that section in the library that represents the animal. As the student points it out to the group, he or she can leave the animal at that location to mark the spot. Use this as a review time to reacquaint students with the library setup.

Step 4: Divide the class up into teams of two or three. Pass out worksheets and go over the directions. Remind the students to look for the animals that mark the places that were covered in your review. Rotate and help where needed.

Closure: Return to the group and share titles.

Wild about
Our Library

Worksheet

Find a book for each category and write the title on the line.

1. Nonfiction _____

2. Reference _____

3. Biography _____

4. Fiction _____

5. Everybody or Easy _____

6. Dr. Seuss Book _____

7. Magazine _____

8. What is the fattest book in the library? _____

Resources for September

Kindergarten and First Grade

Brown, Marc. *D.W.'s Library Card.* Boston: Little, Brown, 2001.

Bruss, Deborah. *Book! Book! Book!* New York: Arthur A. Levine Books, 2001.

Cousins, Lucy. *Maisy Goes to the Library.* Cambridge, MA: Candlewick Press, 2005.

Lehn, Barbara. *What Is a Teacher?* Millbrook, CT: Millbrook Press, 2000.

Murphy, Mary. *Koala and the Flower.* Brookfield, CT: Roaringbrook Press, 2001.

Thompson, Carol. *Mr. Wiggle Looks for Answers.* Columbus, OH: Waterbird Books, 2004.

Thompson, Carol. *Mr. Wiggle Loves to Read.* Columbus, OH: Waterbird Books, 2004.

Thompson, Carol. *Mr. Wiggle's Library.* Columbus, OH: Waterbird Books, 2004.

Second and Third Grade

Colfer, Eoin. *The Legend of Spud Murphy.* New York: Hyperion Books for Children, 2004.

Ernst, Lisa Campbell. *Stella Louella's Runaway Book.* New York: Simon & Schuster Books for Young Readers, 1998.

Kottke, Jan. *A Day with a Librarian.* New York: Children's Press, 2000.

Mora, Pat. *Tomas and the Library Lady.* New York: Alfred A. Knopf, 1997.

Parish, Herman. *Amelia Bedelia, Bookworm.* New York: Greenwillow Books, 2003.

Thaler, Mike. *The Librarian from the Black Lagoon.* New York: Scholastic, 1997.

Williams, Suzanne. *Library Lil.* New York: Dial Books for Young Readers. 1997.

Skeleton Hiccups

By Margery Cuyler

Cuyler, Margery. *Skeleton Hiccups*. New York: Margaret K. McElderry, 2002.

Objective: Students will sequence the events of the story and locate books by six favorite authors on the library shelves.

AASL Standard

Information Literacy

Standard 1: The student who is information literate accesses information efficiently and effectively.

Skills

- Library awareness
- Sequencing

Grade Level: Kindergarten

Materials

- Bar of soap
- Toothbrush
- Cloth
- Pumpkin
- Small rake
- Ball cap
- Spoon
- Water bottle
- Mirror
- One sheet of white construction paper and marker
- Six index cards
- Copy of the call number pattern sheet at the end of this lesson
- Pull from the shelf six books that the students will recognize from these authors: Eric Carle, H.A. Rey, Norman Bridwell, Dr. Seuss, David Kirk, and Rosemary Wells.

Preparing the materials: Write the call number for *Skeleton Hiccups* on the white paper. Make it large enough so it is visible to students. Copy the page of six call numbers, cut apart, glue onto index cards, and laminate.

Step 1: Introduce the story and go over the title and author.

Step 2: Read the story and share the pictures.

Step 3: Line up the items in the wrong order and ask the students to think about where they fit in the story. Ask the students if they are in the correct order. What came first? What came last? Guide them into placing the items in the correct sequence. Page through the book and check for accuracy.

Step 4: Show the front of the book again, and point out the author's name. Hold up the call number on the white construction paper that you have prepared ahead of time. Explain that this book is on the C shelf because we place all of the "Everybody" books according to the author's last name. The E above the C stands for the Everybody section. It is like a house number, and in the library we refer to this as the call number. Long ago, library patrons were unable to go into the stacks, so the call numbers were used to "call out" the location to the librarian who would find it for them. Use the extra books that you have pulled ahead of time to reinforce this concept. Go through the stack, point out the author, and let the students tell on which shelf that book would belong. Using the call number cards you have prepared, match up the call numbers with each of the six books.

Closure: Visit the shelves where these six books are located. Locate those shelves for the students and point out other books by the same author.

Teacher's Notes:

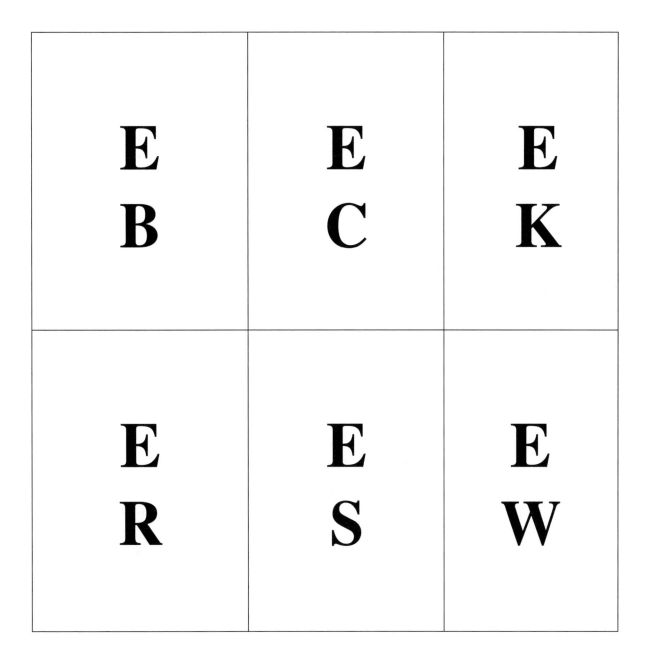

Ten Little Mummies

By Philip Yates

Yates, Philip. *Ten Little Mummies*. New York: Viking, 2003.

Objective: Students will listen to the story and locate books in the Everybody section.

AASL Standard

Information Literacy

Standard 1: The student who is information literate accesses information efficiently and effectively.

Skills

- Library awareness

Grade Level: First grade

Materials

- Call number pattern
- Twenty-six index cards
- Whiteboard and marker
- One nonfiction book from the Nonfiction section
- One made-up story from the Easy/Everybody section
- One made-up story from the Fiction section

Preparing the materials: Copy the call number pages and cut out the individual cards. Paste the call numbers onto index cards and laminate.

Step 1: Before introducing the book, brainstorm a list of things that we count in school. Examples: Lunch tickets, playground equipment, students, and so on. Ask the students why we need to count and keep things in order. Give time for some answers. They will vary with each group.

Step 2: Introduce the book by showing the cover. In this story, we are counting mummies. Read the story and share the pictures.

Step 3: Explain that just like we count to keep track of things in school, we also need to do this in the library. We label each book with a call number, and that helps us locate that book in the library. Some call numbers have just letters, and other have letters and numbers. In the library, we have three kinds of labeling: Easy Fiction, Hard Fiction, and Nonfiction—made-up stories and fact books. Show students both a nonfiction book and two made-up stories, one easy and one fiction. Write the call numbers on the board for all three books that you have pulled from your collection. The Easy/Everybody books have an E and the first letter of the author's last name or some libraries might have the first three letters and the Nonfiction books have a number for the subject and the first three letters of the author's last name. Circle the call number for the easy made-up story and tell students that this is the section you will explore today.

Step 4: Spend time reinforcing the idea that in the library, we keep things in order, and the call number or address on the spine helps us do this. Walk through the Everybody or Easy section pointing out the shelves A to Z. You might want to label the individual shelves ahead of time if this is something you normally do not do at the start of school.

Closure: Seat students on the floor around the shelves of the Everybody section. Using the call number cards that you have prepared ahead of time, call on students one at a time to draw a card and locate the shelf. Play the game until everyone has had a turn.

Teacher's Notes:

Call Number Patterns

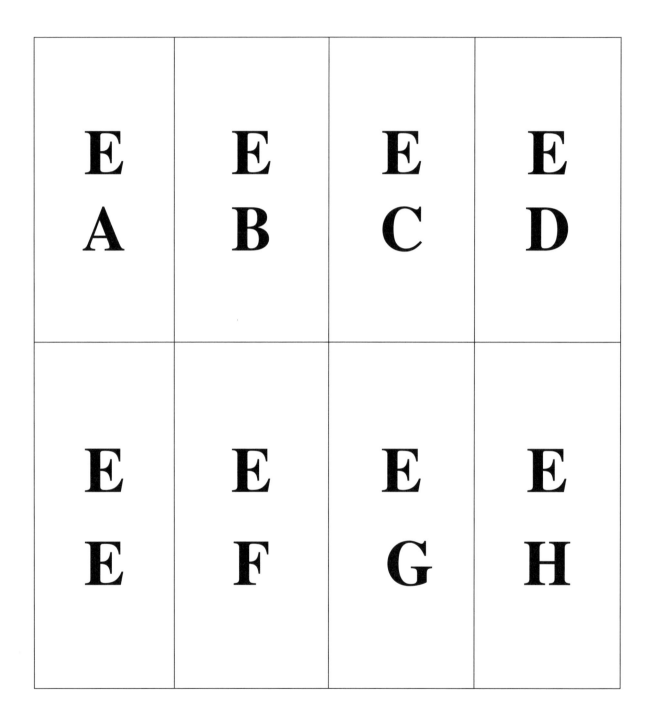

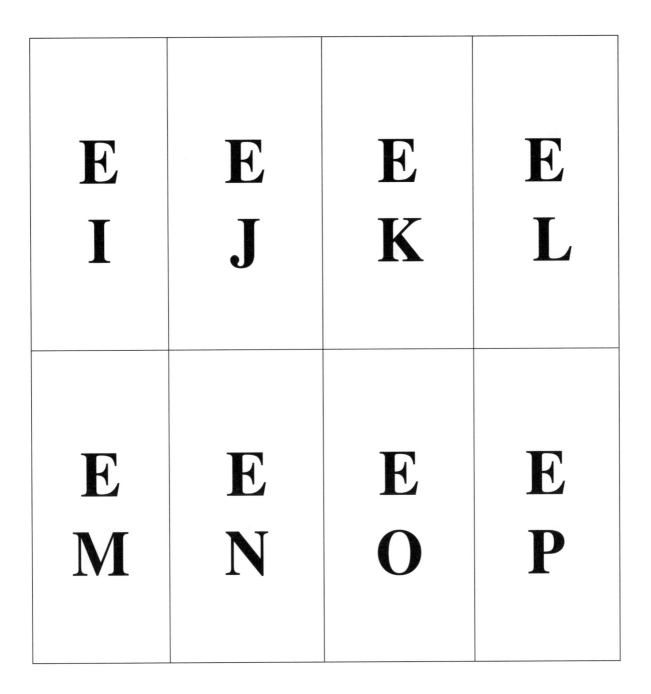

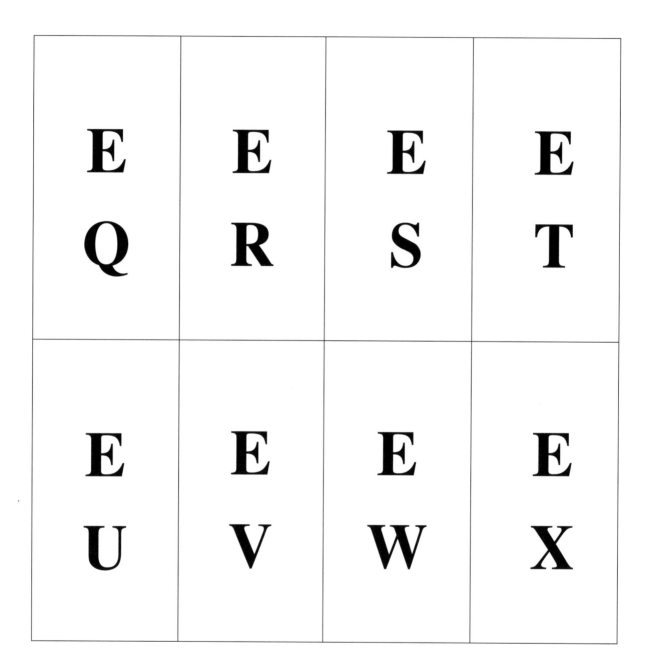

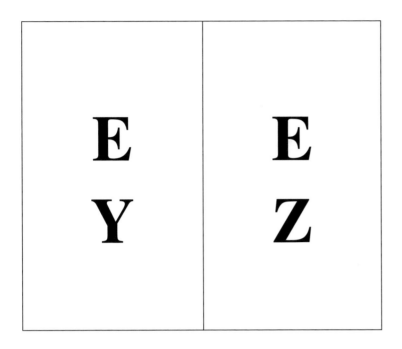

E	E
Y	Z

One Witch

By Laura Leuck

Leuck, Laura. *One Witch.* New York: Walker & Company, 2005.

Objective: Students will listen to the story, compare the sequential numbers in the nonfiction to the numbers in the story, and review the call numbers for easy and nonfiction.

AASL Standard

Information Literacy

Standard 1: The student who is information literate accesses information efficiently and effectively.

Skills

- Arrangement of Easy and Nonfiction sections

Grade Level: Second grade

Materials

- Card stock
- Fifteen nonfiction books with three-digit call numbers
- Fifteen easy books
- Copy of the call numbers from pattern
- An ABC book of your choice (see the resource page at the end of this section of lessons)
- Dry eraser or chalkboard

Preparing the materials: Copy pattern onto card stock. Cut apart and laminate. Write "nonfiction" and "easy" on the board.

Step 1: Introduce the title, author, and illustrator. Talk about the title and cover and ask students what they think the book will be about.

Step 2: Read the first three pages and stop. Ask students to predict what will happen on the next page. Lead students in a short discussion of counting books. Tell students the arrangement of the Nonfiction section is in the form of counting.

Step 3: Finish reading the story. Show the ABC book you have selected, and compare the book to the counting book that the class just heard.

Step 4: Show selection of easy and nonfiction books. Review the difference between easy and nonfiction books.

Step 5: Talk about call numbers as the address of the book. Show examples of call numbers. Discuss the parts of the call number.

Step 6: Sort the example of call numbers into two piles: easy and nonfiction. Give each student an easy or nonfiction book. Have the students sort the selection of books into the correct pile.

Closure: Show students the easy and Nonfiction section on the shelves and the order and arrangement. Students check out books to take home.

Call Number Pattern

E BER	597 PAR
E SHA	031 WOR
E WIL	796 ROT
E HEN	818 ROS

Jeepers Creepers

By Laura Leuck

Leuck, Laura. *Jeepers Creepers: A Monstrous ABC.* San Francisco, CA: Chronicle Books, 2003.

Lesson 1

Objective: Students will listen to the story and review the order of Easy, Fiction, Biography, and Nonfiction books. Students will also write a call number by looking at a fiction author's name or a biography's subject and arranging them in order.

AASL Standard

Information Literacy

Standard 1: The student who is information literate accesses information efficiently and effectively.

Skills

- Arrangement of the Easy, Fiction, Biography, and Nonfiction sections
- Writing call numbers and arranging them in order

Grade Level: Third grade

Materials

- Dry eraser or chalkboard
- Worksheet copied for each student

Preparing the materials: Write "easy," "fiction," "biography," and "nonfiction" on the board.

Step 1: Review the words "easy," "fiction," "biography," and "nonfiction." Ask students what they know about these words. Record responses on the board.

Step 2: Introduce the title, author, and illustrator. Ask the students what they think this book will be about.

Step 3: Read the story, sharing the pictures. Review with students that the order of the Easy and Fiction sections is just like an ABC book, and the books are arranged by the author's last name. Do the same for Nonfiction and Biography sections.

Step 4: Write "Abe Lincoln," "Marc Brown," and "Barbara Park" on the board. Review the parts of a call number. Ask students to help you write call numbers for these authors and subject. Students and teacher can share the writing of the call numbers.

Step 5: Pass out worksheets and pencils. Explain the directions. Allow time for students to complete the worksheet.

Closure: Share and correct worksheets.

Lesson 2

Objective: Students will be able to find books on the shelves using the call numbers of books.

AASL Standard

Information Literacy

Standard 1: The student who is information literate accesses information efficiently and effectively.

Skills

- Library organization

Grade Level: Third grade

Materials

- Call number pattern
- Card stock
- Index cards, one per student
- Pencils

Preparing the materials: Copy the call numbers onto card stock, laminate, and cut apart.

Step 1: Review Lesson 1. Ask students what kind of books are easy, fiction, biography, and non-fiction. What does the call number look like on each of these types of books? What is the order or arrangement of these books on the shelves? Record students' responses on the board.

Step 2: Explain to the students that they are going to look for books using the call numbers.

Step 3: Give each student a pencil and index card. Students need to write an author's name or biography subject from which they would like to select a book. Pass out call numbers and direct students as needed in finding the books.

Closure: After students find call numbers, assist them in the selection of books to check out from their index card.

Teacher's Notes:

Lesson 1

The following authors write easy books. Write the call numbers on the first line, and arrange the call numbers in order by writing a number on the second line.

Eric Carle _____ _____

Norman Bridwell _____ _____

Dr. Seuss _____ _____

Audrey Wood _____ _____

The following authors write fiction books. Write the call numbers on the first line, and arrange the call numbers in order by writing a number on the second line.

Suzy Kline _____ _____

J.K. Rowling _____ _____

Ben Baglio _____ _____

Ron Roy _____ _____

The following names are subjects for biography books. Write the call numbers on the first line, and arrange the call numbers in order by writing a number on the second line.

George Washington _____ _____

Harriet Tubman _____ _____

Benjamin Franklin _____ _____

Hank Aaron _____ _____

Lesson 2

E CAR	E SEU	E WOO	E BRI	E BRO
FIC BAG	FIC ROW	FIC ROY	FIC KLI	FIC PAR
B WAS	B TUB	B FRA	B AAR	B LIN
E COL	E FLE	E WIL	FIC CHR	FIC HAD
B JEF	B MAD	B JOR	B ADA	B WRI

Resources for October

Kindergarten and First Grade

Allen, Susan, and Jane Lindaman. *Read Anything Good Lately?* Minneapolis, MN: Millbrook Press, 2003.

Aylesworth, Jim. *Naughty Little Monkeys.* New York: Dutton Children's Books, 2003.

Bullard, Lisa. *Trick-or-Treat on Milton Street.* Minneapolis, MN: Carolrhoda Books, 2001.

Floca, Brian. *The Racecar Alphabet.* New York: Atheneum Books for Young Readers, 2003.

Mayr, Diane. *Littlebat's Halloween Story.* Morton Grove, IL: Albert Whitman, 2001.

Rose, Deborah Lee. *The Twelve Days of Kindergarten.* New York: Abrams, 2003.

Schulman, Janet. *10 Trick-or-Treaters: A Halloween Counting Book.* New York: Alfred A. Knopf, 2005.

Slate, Joseph. *Miss Bindergarten Plans a Circus with Kindergarten.* New York: Dutton Children's Books, 2002.

Second and Third Grade

Dahl, Michael. *Eggs and Legs: Counting by Twos.* Minneapolis, MN: Picture Window Books, 2005.

Ellis, Rowland-Grey, and Teddy Kentor. *The Scariest Alphabet Book.* Austin, TX: Earin Press, 2002.

Pallotta, Jerry, and Ralph Masiello. *The Skull Alphabet Book.* Watertown, MA: Charlesbridge, 2002.

Schnur, Steven. *Autumn: An Alphabet Acrostic.* New York: Clarion Books, 1997.

The Firefighters' Thanksgiving

By Maribeth Boelts

Boelts, Maribeth. *The Firefighters' Thanksgiving.* New York: G.P. Putnam's Sons, 2004.

Objective: Students will be able to locate favorite books in the library by using the library's specialty spine labels.

AASL Standard

Information Literacy

Standard 1: The student who is information literate accesses information efficiently and effectively.

Skills

- Library awareness
- Sequencing

Grade Level: Kindergarten

Materials

- Six aluminum pie plates
- Pictures for the following: shopping list (list should include the items that are mentioned in the book text), fire hose or firefighter at work putting out a fire, washcloth for cleaning up the trucks, completed Thanksgiving meal, and thank you note from the community (see text).
- Child's play firefighter hat

Preparing the materials: Cut out the pictures and glue them onto the pie plates. On one pie plate, put the title of the book. This will be number one in the sequencing of the story. Also pull examples of books from your library that have special labels on the spine to represent types of books such as Christmas, Thanksgiving, cats, dogs, and so on. These can be purchased from a library supply catalog such as The Library Store, or the students can make them. Most elementary libraries have these spine stickers to help younger patrons locate favorites more easily.

Step 1: Share the front of the book, and before reading the title, ask students to predict what the story will be about. Give some time for student comments. The colorful picture of the fire truck should excite the kindergarteners and many comments will follow.

Step 2: Read the story and share the pictures.

Step 3: Show the pie plates to the students and explain that these have pictures that represent different parts of today's story. Line them up so that they are not in the correct order. Spend time calling on students to put the next plate in order as you retell the story. You might need to ask questions such as, "What happened next to the firefighters?" It is important for the students to understand why the firefighters were unable to finish the dinner that they planned to cook. Page through the story so that corrections can be made for any problems in the sequencing process.

Step 4: (Move your students to the Everybody section if your story corner is not nearby.) Using the books that you have pulled as examples, stress the use of spine label pictures that we have in the library and how they help us locate books that are all related to a similar topic. Example: Thanksgiving books are all labeled with a turkey. Compare the spine of the book to people's spines. Stress how our spines hold us up so that we can stand up tall. Ask a student to stand up and point out his or her spine. Ask students to feel for their own spines. Explain each spine label that you have in the library. These will vary with each elementary library. As you show that label, ask a student to put on the firefighter hat and go to the shelves and find another book that has the same sticker. The student should bring the book back to share with the group. Read the title and share the front of the book. Once you have shown all of the books and stickers, continue by calling on students until everyone has had a turn locating a book. Example: "I need a cat book. Mary bring one back to the circle."

Closure: Give students time to locate a book to check out. Ask them to find a favorite book using the spine labels.

Teacher's Notes:

Thank You, Thanksgiving

By David Milgrim

Milgrim, David. *Thank You, Thanksgiving.* New York: Clarion Books, 2003.

Objective: Students will listen to the story, identify author and illustrator, and practice being an author and illustrator.

AASL Standard

Information Literacy

Standard 1: The student who is information literate accesses information efficiently and effectively.

Skills

- Author and illustrator
- Creative writing

Grade Level: First grade

Materials

- Copies of worksheets
- Copy of word cards
- Crayons and pencils
- Dry eraser or chalkboard

Preparing the materials: Copy worksheets for each student. Then make three copies of the second one. Then cut and staple together to create a book. Copy word cards, cut them out, and laminate.

Step 1: Show the words "author" and "illustrator" as you introduce the concepts. Tell the students that the author writes the words and the illustrator makes the pictures in a book.

Step 2: Introduce the title and author of the book. Tell the students that in this book the author and illustrator is the same person. Write the author's name on the board.

Step 3: Read the story and share the pictures.

Step 4: Record on the board all the things the girl in the book is thankful for.

Step 5: Pass out copies of the stapled books. Tell students they are going to practice being an author and an illustrator.

Step 6: Model on the board the writing of the students' names on the front cover of their book.

Step 7: Tell students to fill in the blanks with the things they are thankful for and to draw a picture on each page.

Closure: Share stories, review the words "author" and "illustrator," and check out books.

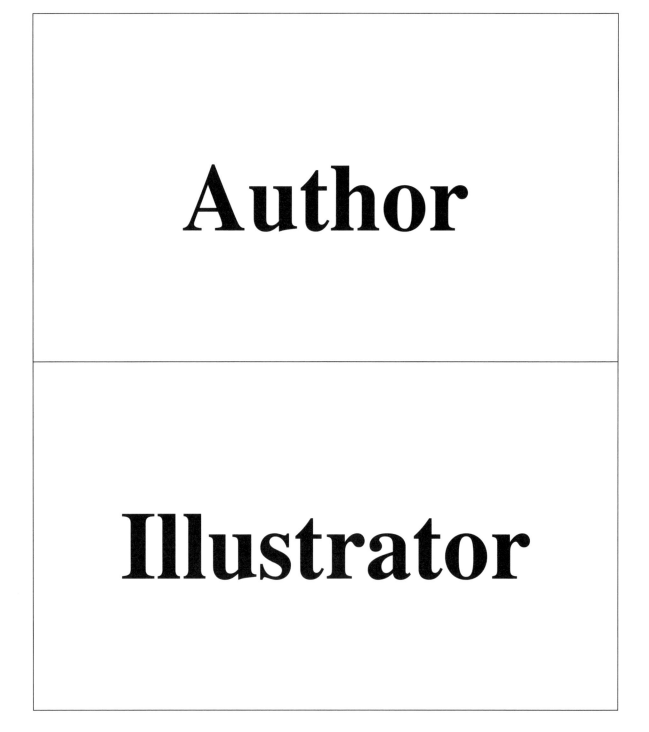

Author

Illustrator

Thank You, Thanksgiving
By

_____

- -

Thank you, _____.

Thank You,_____.

- -

Thank you, _____.

From *A Year in Picture Books: Linking to the Information Literacy Standards* by Patricia A. Messner and Brenda S. Copeland. Westport, CT: Libraries Unlimited. Copyright © 2007 Patricia A. Messner and Brenda S. Copeland.

Thank You,_____.

- -

Thank you, Thanksgiving.

Turkey Surprise

By Peggy Archer

Archer, Peggy. *Turkey Surprise*. New York: Dial Books for Young Readers, 2005.

Objective: Students will listen and participate in the story and identify the author, illustrator, and title on the cover and on the title page of the book.

AASL Standards

Information Literacy

Standard 3: The student who is information literate uses information accurately and creatively.

Independent Learning

Standard 5: The student who is an independent learner is information literate and appreciates literature and other creative expressions of information.

Skills

- Choral reading
- Author, illustrator, and title recognition
- Reading encouragement

Grade Level: First grade

Materials

- An assortment of books with the title, author, and illustrator on the cover (enough for one per student)
- Fifteen pilgrim hats and fifteen feathers (purchased at a craft store)
- Chart paper
- Marker
- Two pointers
- Fifteen paint sticks

Preparing the materials: Write the song the pilgrims sang on a piece of chart paper. Write the phrase the turkey speaks (Where, oh where, can I hide?) on another piece of chart paper. You might want to laminate the chart paper for longer use. Using the pilgrim hat pattern and paint sticks make fifteen pilgrim puppets. Copy pattern onto card stock, laminate, and attach to the paint stick with tape.

Step 1: Review the author and illustrator from the previous lesson. Introduce the word "title." Write "title" on the board. Introduce the title, author, and illustrator of *Turkey Surprise.*

Step 2: Give every student a pilgrim hat puppet or a feather. Have the pilgrim puppets sit together and the feather students sit together.

Step 3: Explain the choral reading parts for the pilgrims and the turkeys. Show the chart paper, and select a head pilgrim and a head turkey. The head pilgrim and head turkey will point to the choral reading when the time is right. Practice reading the phrases together before reading the story.

Step 4: Read the story and give students the opportunity to participate at appropriate times.

Closure: Pass out selected books and have students find the author, title, and illustrator on the outside of their books. Students check out books.

Teacher's Notes:

Pilgrim Hat Pattern

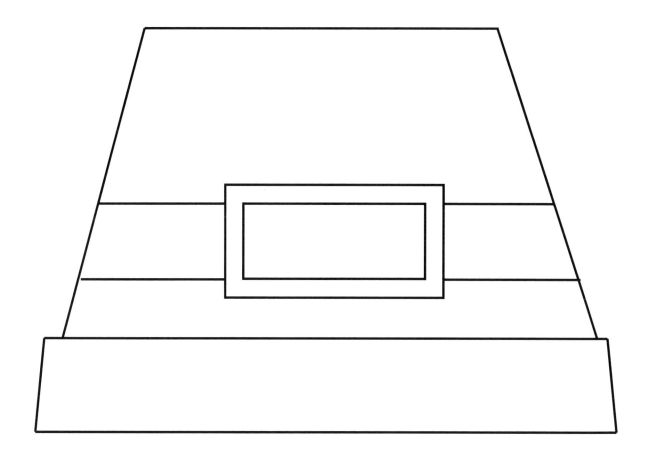

The Hello, Goodbye Window

Written by Norton Juster
Illustrated by Chris Raschka

Juster, Norton. *The Hello, Goodbye Window*. New York: Hyperion Books for Children, 2005.

Objective: Students will listen to a Caldecott Award–winning book, become familiar with the award, answer comprehension questions, and search for other Caldecott titles.

AASL Standards

Information Literacy

Standard 1: The student who is information literate accesses information efficiently and effectively.

Standard 2: The student who is information literate evaluates information critically and competently.

Skills

- Reading encouragement

- Recognizing Caldecott Award winners

- Comprehension

Grade Level: Second grade

Materials

- A Caldecott poster (many companies give these out free)

- A selection of Caldecott Medal and Honor books

- Window pattern

- Shoebox without the lid

- A piece of leftover laminating film

- Brown crayon

Preparing the materials: Copy window pattern onto card stock, write the comprehension questions on windows, cut them out, and laminate. Enlarge one window onto card stock to fit on the top of the shoebox; cut out around the window and around the inside of the window. Color the window brown. Tape the leftover laminating film to the top half of the window, leaving the bottom half open. Attach the window to the shoe box, and insert the windows with the questions into the shoe box. See diagram. Display the poster and books so all students can view them.

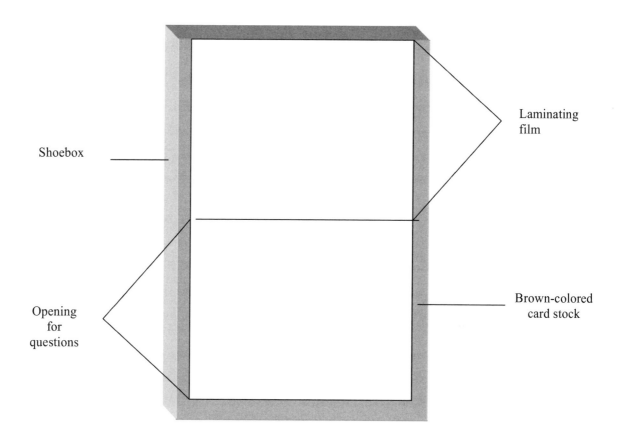

Step 1: Discuss the Caldecott Award with students using the poster and books as visual displays.

Step 2: Demonstrate (by showing books) to students that the first-place and Honor Books are usually marked in identifiable ways, with a gold or silver seal. Explain that sometimes libraries use a special spine label to identify winners. Make sure to show students how these books are identified in your library.

Step 3: Introduce *The Hello, Goodbye Window* written by Norton Juster and illustrated by Chris Raschka. Remind the students that this book was a winner for its illustrations.

Step 4: Read the story and share the pictures.

Step 5: Using the questions you have placed in the shoebox, ask students to take turns reading and answering the questions.

Closure: Remind students about the special label for the Caldecott Medal winners. Help students find other Caldecott books on the shelves. Students check out books to take home.

Teacher's Notes:

Comprehension Questions and Activities Labeled with Bloom's Levels of Thinking Taxonomy

Knowledge

Why did the little girl stay with her grandparents during the day?

What were some of the things the little girl did while staying at her grandparents' house?

In what room is the "Hello, Goodbye Window"?

What did the little girl and her grandparents do as they looked out the window?

Comprehension

Summarize your favorite part of the story.

Describe your favorite illustration.

Summarize the funniest part.

Application

Why did the little girl enjoy staying with her grandparents?

In your opinion, how old was the little girl?

Why did the author title the book *The Hello, Goodbye Window?*

Does the Queen of England ever come and visit? Why or why not?

Window Pattern

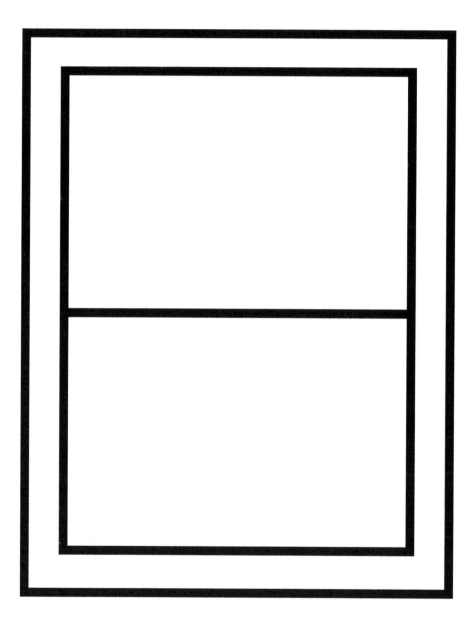

Rosa

By Nikki Giovanni

Giovanni, Nikki. *Rosa.* New York: Henry Holt, 2005.

Objective: Students will listen to the story and write descriptive words.

AASL Standard

Information Literacy

Standard 7: The student who contributes positively to the learning community and to society is information literate and recognizes the importance of information to a democratic society.

Skills

- Recognizing Coretta Scott King Award Winners
- Main character study

Grade Level: Third grade

Materials

- Books and magazines article about Rosa Parks
- Pictures of Rosa Parks

Preparing the materials: Pull books that are related to Rosa Parks. Create a display for student interest for further reading opportunities. Visit the following ALA Web site for background information on the Coretta Scott King Award: http://www.ala.org//ala/emiert/ corettascottkingbookawards/corettascott.htm.

Step 1: Introduce the story by giving some brief comments about why this book was chosen for the Coretta Scott King Award. Explain who can receive this award and why it is given.

Step 2: Read the story and ask students to listen for important characteristics about Rosa Parks.

Step 3: Call on students to explain what they know about Rosa from reading the story. Write these on the board. Ask students to identify passages in the text that support the statement. Review parts of the story as needed.

Step 4: Pass out worksheets and discuss the directions. The statements on the board will help the students write adjectives to describe the main character. You may have to teach a short lesson about adjectives. Show an example so they can understand the assignment.

Examples:

Rosa worked in the sewing department.—Good seamstress, excellent seamstress, or other adjectives

She skipped lunch to finish a job.—Dedicated

Closure: Give students time to share as a whole group. Record adjectives next to the statements on the board. Review the reason this was a special award book. Encourage students to visit the reading center containing other material on Rosa Parks.

What special adjectives describe Rosa Parks?
Write these inside the windows of the bus.

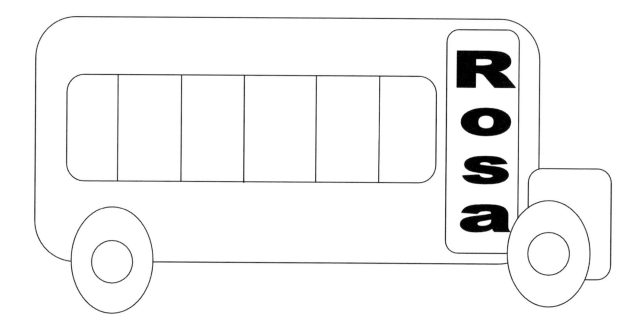

Rosa by Nikki Giovanni received the 2005 _____

_____

Award.

This book was special because_____

_____.

Resources for November

Thanksgiving Books

Atwell, Debby. *The Thanksgiving Door.* Boston: Houghton Mifflin, 2003.

Herman, Charlotte. *The Memory Cupboard.* Morton Grove, IL: Whitman, 2003.

Hines, Gary. *Thanksgiving in the White House.* New York: Henry Holt, 2003.

Kimmelman, Leslie. *Round the Turkey: A Grateful Thanksgiving.* Morton Grove, IL: Whitman, 2002.

Spinelli, Eileen. *The Perfect Thanksgiving.* New York: Henry Holt, 2003.

Caldecott Award Books

Gerstein, Mordicai. *The Man Who Walked between the Towers.* Brookfield, CT: Roaring Brook Press, 2003.

Henkes, Kevin. *Kitten's First Full Moon.* New York: HarperCollins, 2004.

Coretta Scott King Award Books

Holiday, Billie, and Arthur Hernog Jr. *God Bless the Child.* New York: HarperCollins, 2003.

Shange, Ntozake. *Ellington Was Not a Street.* New York: Simon & Schuster Books for Young Readers, 2004.

I Wish Santa Would Come by Helicopter

By Harriet Ziefert

Ziefert, Harriet. *I Wish Santa Would Come by Helicopter.* New York: Sterling Publishing Co., 2004.

Lesson 1

Objective: Students will understand what information is and the many forms of information.

AASL Standards

Information Literacy

Standard 1: The student who is information literate accesses information efficiently and effectively.

Standard 3: The student who is information literate uses information accurately and creatively.

Skills

- Understanding information

Grade Level: Kindergarten

Materials

- Copy of word cards
- Card stock
- Pictures of examples of transportation
- CD of transportation sounds (*The Ultimate Digital-Stereo Library Sound Effects. Universal City, California: Empire Musicwerks, Inc., 2005.*)
- CD player
- Silk flower
- Dry eraser or chalkboard

Preparing the materials: Copy words and definitions onto card stock, cut out, and laminate.

Step 1: Ask the question, "How does Santa travel?" Students will probably answer in a sled. Ask another question such as, "How does he get to the mall?" Hopefully, the children will say by car, train, or bus. Lead class in a discussion of the many ways Santa could travel.

Step 2: Introduce the title and author. Read story and discuss pictures.

Step 3: Using word cards for information and the flower, talk about what information is. Tell students information is facts or true things about something. Show students the flower, and write the word flower on the board. Ask the students to give a fact about the flower. Example: The flower is yellow. Write the word "yellow" on the board under the word "flower."

Continue to write words on the board. Measure the flower and record the inches on the board with the other words. Tell students that all the words you wrote on the board are information about the flower.

Step 4: Tell students that we can get information different ways just like Santa comes in different ways. Use the word cards and show the pictures of transportation and listen to the sound effects on the CD. Discuss the kinds of information found on the CD and record on the board. Examples: Motor sounds, rotor blades touching, etc.

Closure: Review the word cards and the different ways that we get information.

Lesson 2

Objective: Students will listen to a nonfiction book about helicopters and afterward recall facts.

AASL Standards

Information Literacy

Standard 1: The student who is information literate accesses information efficiently and effectively.

Standard 3: The student who is information literate uses information accurately and creatively.

Skills

- Finding information

Grade Level: Kindergarten

Materials

- A nonfiction book about helicopters (example: Richardson, Adele D. *Transport Helicopters.* Mankato, MN: Bridgestone Books, 2001)
- CD of sound effects from Lesson 1
- Word cards from Lesson 1
- Helicopter rotors pattern

Preparing the materials: Using the pattern, make an overhead.

Step 1: Review the word "information" and its definition. Remind students of the flower from Lesson 1 and the information we collected.

Step 2: Introduce the nonfiction book and tell students that we are going to find information about helicopters. We are going to look at three different ways to find information: words, pictures, and sounds.

Step 3: Read the nonfiction book about helicopters.

Step 4: Using the overhead, have students recall information from the words and pictures.

Step 5: Listen to the CD of sound effects and help students find information about helicopters and add those to the overhead.

Closure: Review with students that they can find information in at least three different ways: words, pictures, sounds; then suggest that they can find information through smell and touch as well. Students check out books to take home.

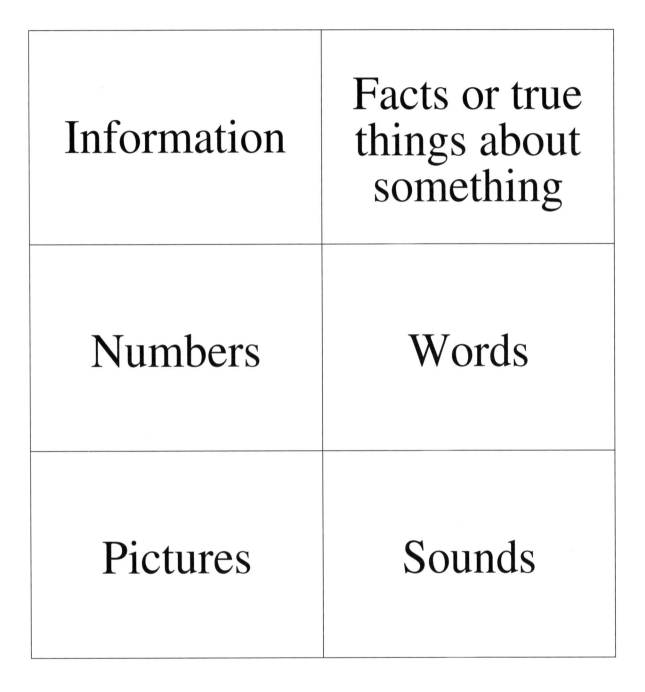

Information	Facts or true things about something
Numbers	Words
Pictures	Sounds

Rotors Overhead Pattern

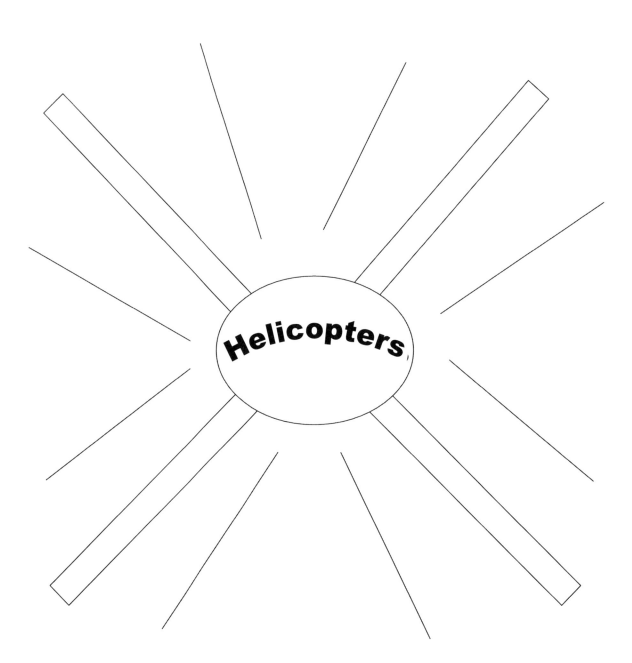

Snowmen at Christmas

By Caralyn Buehner

Buehner, Caralyn. *Snowmen at Christmas*. New York: Dial Books for Young Readers, 2005.

Objective: Students will listen to the story and sequence the main events. Students will make a list of winter activities that appear in the story using picture and word clues.

AASL Standard

Information Literacy

Standard 3: The student who is information literate uses information accurately and creatively.

Skills

- Information gathering of text and picture clues
- Setting
- Sequencing

Grade Level: First grade

Materials

- Snowman overhead
- Snowman worksheet

Step 1: Introduce the story by sharing the front cover of the book and review where books by this author are located on your library shelf. Write the call number on the board to reinforce this concept.

Step 2: Read the story and ask students to look for clues in the text and pictures that tell the reader what the setting is for this story. Review what we mean by the "setting" of a story if your group is not familiar with the term.

Step 3: Start the discussion by asking where this story takes place. Do we have snow at Christmas where we live? Where in the United States would they not have snow? Build on this discussion by asking what clues in the story tell us that it is wintertime. Record the students' comments on the overhead. Reread text passages if necessary to include things such as, snow mothers made iced sweets. Students will start with the obvious clues, but the teacher should move to the harder text clues as the discussion comes to an end.

Closure: Give out the worksheet on sequencing and go over the directions. Give students time to complete. Correct together if time permits.

Put the main events in order by placing a number inside the buttons.

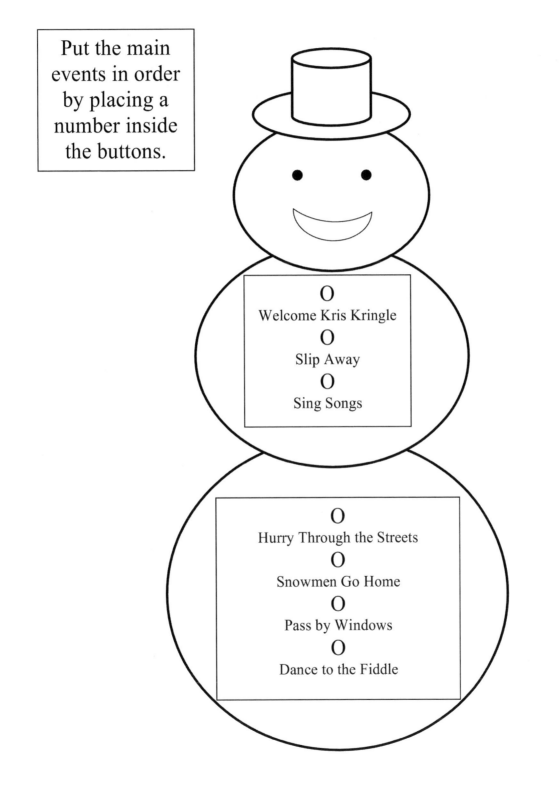

O
Welcome Kris Kringle
O
Slip Away
O
Sing Songs

O
Hurry Through the Streets
O
Snowmen Go Home
O
Pass by Windows
O
Dance to the Fiddle

Why Is It Snowing?

By Judith A. Williams

Williams, Judith A. *Why Is It Snowing?* Berkeley Heights, NJ: Enslow, 2005.

Objective: Students will listen to the story and make a list of facts about snow.

AASL Standard

Information Literacy

Standard 3: The student who is information literate uses information accurately and creatively.

Skills

- Information gathering

Grade Level: First grade

Materials

- Snow overhead

Step 1: Introduce the story by sharing the front cover of the book and ask students to speculate what this book is about. Ask if this is a nonfiction or a fiction book. Why or why not?

Step 2: Before reading the story, ask students what are "facts"? Discuss with students that facts are real information about real things. Ask the students to listen for facts in the story about snow.

Step 3: Read the story. Using the overhead, ask the students for facts from the book that we learned from today's story. Record these on the snow blocks.

Closure: Walk the students through the 500s of the Nonfiction section and discuss with them why you are in this section. Snow is weather and the weather books are in the 500s. Book talk books from this section.

Teacher's Notes:

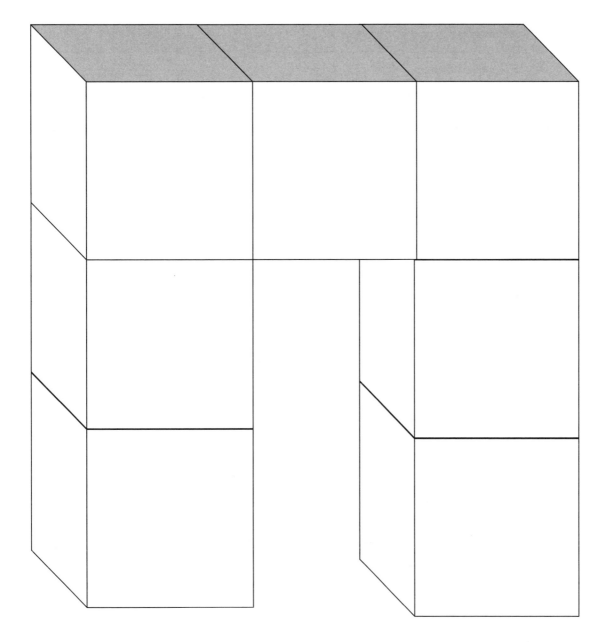

The Three Bears' Christmas

By Kathy Duval

Duval, Kathy. *The Three Bears' Christmas*. New York: Holiday House, 2005.

Lesson 1

Objective: Students will listen to a fiction and nonfiction book and compare and contrast using a Venn diagram.

AASL Standards

Information Literacy

Standard 1: The student who is information literate accesses information efficiently and effectively.

Standard 3: The student who is information literate uses information accurately and creatively.

Skills

- Compare and contrast

- Understand fiction versus nonfiction (fact versus fiction)

Grade Level: Second grade

Materials

- Venn diagram pattern made into an overhead

- A nonfiction book about bears

- Dry eraser or chalkboard

- Marker or chalk

Step 1: Review words fact and fiction. Write words on the board and have students tell you what they mean. Introduce fiction and nonfiction as sections in the library. Write the words "fiction" and "nonfiction" on the board.

Step 2: Tell students they will read two books today, one fiction and one nonfiction. After the reading, we will compare and contrast the two books.

Step 3: Introduce the book, *The Three Bears' Christmas*. Ask the students if it is a fiction or nonfiction book. Students should respond with appropriate reasons why this is a fiction book.

Step 4: Read book and share the pictures.

Step 5: Introduce a nonfiction book about bears and ask the students if this is a fiction or nonfiction book. Read the book and share the pictures and captions.

Step 6: Using the Venn diagram overhead, have students recall information from each book and record in the correct place.

Closure: Show students the nonfiction bear books on the shelves. Student check out books to take home.

Lesson 2

Objective: Students will create puppets and props to retell the fiction and nonfiction books about bears.

AASL Standards

Information Literacy

Standard 1: The student who is information literate accesses information efficiently and effectively.

Standard 3: The student who is information literate uses information accurately and creatively.

Skills

- Understanding information
- Using information creatively

Grade Level: Second grade

Materials

- A copy of the book *The Three Bears' Christmas*
- A copy of the story "The Three Bears"
- A copy of the nonfiction book of bears used in the first lesson
- Another nonfiction book about bears
- Scrap construction paper
- Scissors
- Crayons and pencils
- Glue
- Bear puppet pattern copied for each group
- Paint sticks (free at a paint store)

Step 1: Explain to students that they are going to work in groups. Each group will have a book to read, make puppets and props, and retell the information to the rest of the class.

Step 2: Divide class into four groups. Give each group a book and copies of the bear puppet.

Step 3: Tell students to read the book and make a list of puppets and props. The nonfiction book might just need one bear puppet to retell the information. Students decide as a group what information the group will tell the class.

Step 4: Allow time for students to complete puppets and props.

Closure: Students check out books to take home.

Lesson 3

Objective: Students will share their puppets, props, facts, and/or story with the class.

AASL Standards

Information Literacy

Standard 1: The student who is information literate accesses information efficiently and effectively.

Standard 3: The student who is information literate uses information accurately and creatively.

Skills

- Using information creatively

Grade Level: Second grade

Materials

- A puppet stage (a table with a sheet works fine)

Step 1: Students share the facts or story using their puppets and props.

Step 2: Allow time for all groups to share.

Closure: Students check out books to take home.

Teacher's Notes:

Lesson 1

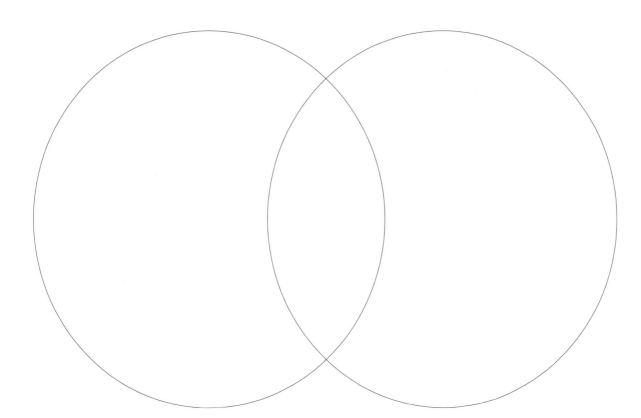

The Three
Bears' Christmas

Title of Book

_____

Lesson 2

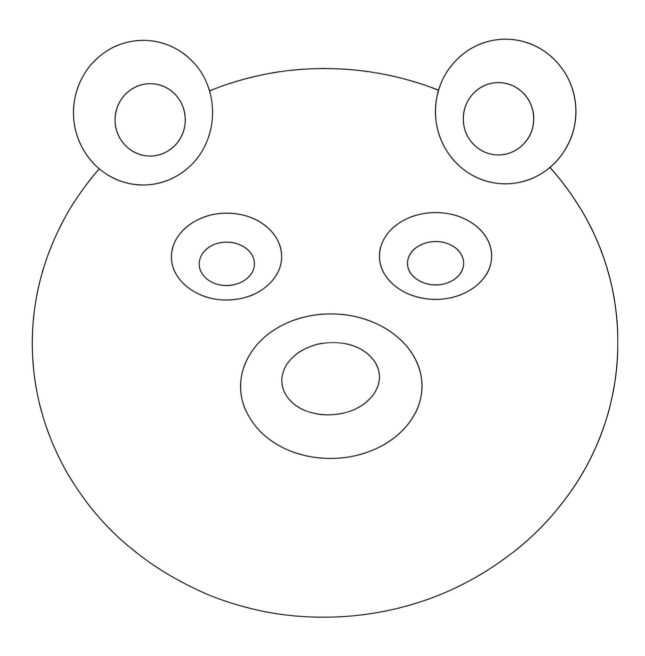

An Orange for Frankie

By Patricia Polacco

Polacco, Patricia. *An Orange for Frankie.* New York: Philomel Books, 2004.

Lesson 1

Objective: Students will listen to the story and write a descriptive paragraph about one of their own family traditions.

AASL Standards

Information Literacy

Standard 1: The student who is information literate accesses information efficiently and effectively.

Standard 3: The student who is information literate uses information accurately and creatively.

Independent Learning

Standard 4: The student who is an independent learner is information literate and pursues information related to personal interests.

Social Responsibility

Standard 9: The student who contributes positively to the learning community and to society is information literate and participates effectively in groups to pursue and generate information.

Skills

- Shared writing

Grade Level: Third grade

Materials

- A large orange
- Orange picture overhead
- Lunch-size paper bag
- Orange worksheet
- Dictionary

Preparing the materials: Place the orange inside a lunch-size paper bag

Step 1: Before showing the book, ask a student to come forward to the front of the class and close his or her eyes. Have the student smell the contents of the bag and tell the class what is inside. If the student is unable to decide that it is an orange, ask him or her to reach inside and feel the item and then decide what it is.

Step 2: Share the front of the book and read the title and author. Explain that this story is about a family tradition, and ask students to listen for clues that will help write a definition at the end of the lesson.

Step 3: Read the story and share the pictures.

Step 4: Using the overhead transparency provided, ask students to help write a definition on the orange displayed on the overhead.

Closure: Pick a student to look up the word "tradition" in the dictionary and read the definition to the class. Compare the dictionary definition to the one that the students wrote. Give out a copy of the orange worksheet so that students can write about a family Christmas tradition at their house. Partner share if time permits.

Lesson 2

Objective: Students will research a holiday tradition or celebration from another country.

AASL Standards

Information Literacy

Standard 1: The student who is information literate accesses information efficiently and effectively.
Standard 3: The student who is information literate uses information accurately and creatively.

Independent Learning

Standard 4: The student who is an independent learner is information literate and pursues information related to personal interests.

Skills

- Research

Grade Level: Third grade

Materials

- Collection of books about other countries and holiday traditions
- Worksheet for each group

Step 1: Review the story and the definition of tradition from last week's lesson.

Step 2: Show the books that you have collected and briefly explain that there are many different holiday celebrations and traditions celebrated at this time of the year, both in the United States and around the world.

Step 3: Read and share a couple of examples from the books that you have collected. Brainstorm words that students could use to check in the index to locate needed information (examples: festival, holiday, celebration).

Step 4: Hand out the worksheet and go over the directions. Stress that the students need to cite the source they are using: recording both the title and author. Divide up students according to the amount of materials in your collection of countries and holiday traditions books.

Step 5: Dismiss students to work independently and help where needed.

Closure: Return to the large group and share information. (You may wish to continue and work on this another class period if students have trouble completing this task.)

A tradition is

_____

_____

_____

_____

_____

My Family Tradition

Holiday Traditions and Celebrations around the World

Read about another country's traditions and celebrations. Fill in the blanks below.

Name of Celebration_____

Country_____

Food Served_____

Time of Celebration _____

List Two Awesome Facts about the Tradition:

1._____

_____

_____

2._____

_____

_____

Source of Information:

Title_____

Author_____

Resources for December

Kindergarten and First Grade

Brett, Jan. *Who's That Knocking on Christmas Eve?* New York: G.P. Putnam, 2002.

Bunting, Eve. *One Candle.* New York: Joanna Cotler Books/HarperCollins, 2002.

Chocolate, Deborah M. Newton. *My First Kwanzaa Book.* New York: Scholastic, 1999.

Climo, Shirley. *Cobweb Christmas.* New York: HarperCollins, 2001.

Kirk, David. *Dashing through the Snow.* New York: Callaway, 2005.

Wilson, Karma. *Bear Stays Up for Christmas.* New York: Margaret K. McElderry Books, 2004.

Wood, Don, and Audrey Wood. *Merry Christmas, Big Hungry Bear!* New York: Blue Sky Press, 2002.

Second and Third Grade

Appelt, Kathi. *Merry Christmas, Merry Crow.* New York: Harcourt, 2005.

Bond, Rebecca. *A City Christmas Tree.* New York: Little, Brown and Company, 2005.

McKissack, Patricia C. *Messy Bessey's Holidays.* New York: Scholastic, 2001.

Medearis, Angela Shelf. *Seven Spools of Thread.* New York: Scholastic, 2005.

Polacco, Patricia. *Christmas Tapestry.* New York: Philomel Books, 2002.

Polacco, Patricia. *The Trees of the Dancing Goats.* New York: Aladdin Paperbacks, 2000.

The First Day of Winter

By Denise Fleming

Fleming, Denise. *The First Day of Winter.* New York: Henry Holt, 2005.

Objective: Students will listen and participate in the story. Students will find books on the shelves using the first letter of the author's last name.

AASL Standards

Information Literacy

Standard 1: The student who is information literate accesses information efficiently and effectively.

Standard 3: The student who is information literate uses information accurately and creatively.

Independent Learning

Standard 5: The student who is an independent learner is information literate and appreciates literature and other creative expressions of information.

Skills

- Reading encouragement
- Using information creatively
- Library organization

Grade Level: Kindergarten

Materials

- Red cap
- Two blue mittens
- Three striped scarves
- Four pinecones
- Five packages of seeds
- Five pieces of felt
- Six twigs
- Seven maple leaves
- Eight orange berries
- Nine black buttons
- Ten peanuts

- Spinc label pattern
- A book for each spine label

Preparing the materials: Copy the spine label pattern onto card stock, cut out, and laminate.

Step 1: Introduce the title and author. Read the story and share pictures.

Step 2: Pass out props and reread the story. As you reread the story, the students will hold up their prop at the correct time and say the correct phrase. Example: One red cap or two blue mittens.

Step 3: Tell the students that this book is like a counting book, and it is in numerical, or numbered, order. Say, "Remember that our books are in order on our shelves. The Easy/Everybody section is in ABC order by the author's last name."

Step 4: Show the front of the book *The First Day of Winter.* Ask students to point out the title and the author.

Step 5: Looking at the author's name on the card, ask students under what letter this book would be found. Show spine label card and spine label of the book.

Step 6: Divide class into six groups. Tell the students they are going to look for books by the author's last name. Show spine label card, author card and matching book. Give each group a card and book. Have students look for their books in the Easy/Everybody section. Assist those who need extra help.

Closure: All groups will show the rest of the class where they found their books.

Teacher's Notes:

E F	E C	E S	E W
E B	E C	Denise Fleming	Eric Carle
David Shannon	Audrey Wood	Marc Brown	Donald Crews

All You Need for a Snowman

By Alice Schertle

Schertle, Alice. *All You Need for a Snowman*. New York: Harcourt, 2002.

Objective: Students will listen to the story and put the snowman together in order as it happens in the story.

AASL Standards

Information Literacy

Standard 2: The student who is information literate evaluates information critically and competently.

Standard 3: The student who is information literate uses information accurately and creatively.

Skills

- Sequencing

- Nonfiction and Fiction

Grade Level: First grade

Materials

- Three sheets of while plastic craft material

- One sheet of green plastic craft material

- Ribbon or plastic flowers for hat

- Package of plastic snowflakes

- Two bottle caps

- Plastic carrot

- Five walnuts

- An old belt cut down so that the buckle and part of the belt can be used

- One pair of doll or teddy-bear boots

- Wool scarf

- Mittens

- Earmuffs

- Fanny pack

- Small broom from a craft store

- Collection of nonfiction books

Preparing the materials: Cut out three white circles: 12 inches, 8 inches, and 6 inches in diameter. Use the green plastic and the hat pattern to create a hat for the snowman. Decorate the hat with ribbon or a flower.

Step 1: Share the front of the book, and read the title and author. Ask students to predict what the story will be about, giving time for answers.

Step 2: Read the story and share the pictures with the class.

Step 3: Give out the things that you have collected, making sure that each child has a piece to work with when you build the snowman.

Step 4: Go back and retell the story, giving the students the opportunity to help by building the snowman on the floor in front of the class. Check the book at the end to see if the sequencing was correct.

Step 5: Ask the students if this was a fiction or a nonfiction story. Make a T chart on the board, and put "Fiction" on one side and "Nonfiction" on the other. List the picture clues and text clues that helped the students with this process.

Step 6: Give out the collection of nonfiction books. Give students time to page through the books. Explain that these books are all nonfiction. Help the class list the things that tell us that these books are nonfiction (examples: facts, photos, table of contents, etc.).

Closure: Review the chart and help students select a nonfiction book to take home to share with their families.

Teacher's Notes:

Hat Pattern

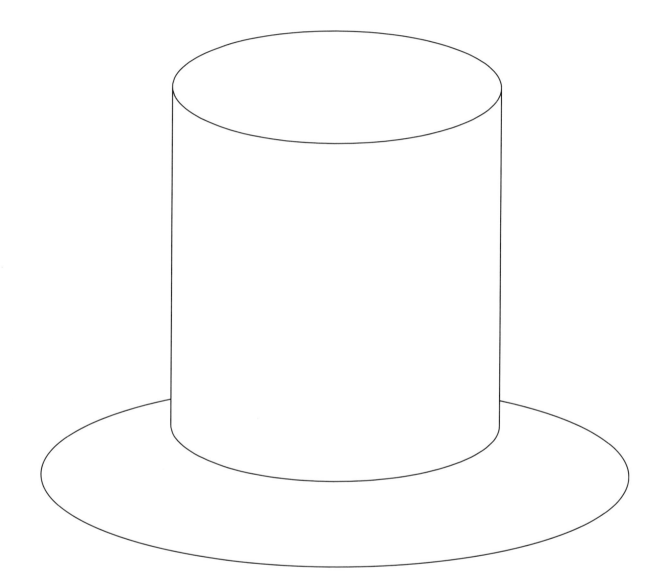

Coming On Home Soon

By Jacqueline Woodson

Woodson, Jacqueline. *Coming On Home Soon.* New York: G.P. Putnam, 2004.

Objective: Students will listen to the story and sort a collection of books into fiction and nonfiction using the call numbers on the spine.

AASL Standards

Information Literacy

Standard 2: The student who is information literate evaluates information critically and competently.

Standard 3: The student who is information literate uses information accurately and creatively.

Skills

- Fiction and nonfiction sorting

Grade Level: Second grade

Materials

- Collection of nonfiction books from the 624s. (Mama in the story goes to Chicago to take a job cleaning trains, so this is a good section to tie into the story.)

- Collection of books from the Everybody section similar to the book in the lesson. (Pick ones that are around a theme such as Black History or that are more realistic in nature. Example: books written by Eve Bunting.) We want students to learn to use the call number on the spine to decide if the book is fiction or nonfiction. Choose ones that will make this task harder. In other words, no animal stories wearing people clothes.

Preparing the materials: Mix the collection of books together. Write the words nonfiction and fiction on the board.

Step 1: Since January is Black History month, we have chosen this realistic story about a black family. It will create great discussion among your young readers, and you might wish to create a group of questions to go along with this book for class discussion.

Step 2: Introduce the book by pointing out the title and author first. Ask the students to decide at the end of the story if this is a nonfiction or a fiction book. Read the story and share the pictures. Could this story really happen? How do we decide if this is true or made up?

Step 3: Review the terms nonfiction and fiction with the class. Because of the realistic nature of the story the students will have a hard time deciding if this is real or not. Explain that in the library we have the call numbers labeled on the spine so we can tell where the book belongs. Copy the call number of the book on the board and review with the students how the E stands for everybody and the letter under the E stands for the author's last name. These are made-up stories even though they sound real. We call these stories fiction. Share one of the nonfiction books that you have pulled ahead of time. Write the call number on the board, and explain that all of the train books have the same call number. All nonfiction or fact books have a number on the spine. All of the books about a special topic have the same call number.

Step 4: Work through the pile of books, reading the call numbers or writing them on the board, and let the students sort books into two piles, fiction and nonfiction.

Closure: Walk the students through the 600s, pointing out where these books would be located on the shelf.

Optional Activity: Student fun worksheet (see following page).

Teacher's Notes:

Find the words below in the word search and answer the questions at the bottom of the page.

Word box

Ada Ruth	Grandma	Letters	Work	Love
Mama	Chicago	Train	Money	Snow

```
A D A R U T H K
A M D N A R G I
S R E T T E L T
L J K R O W L T
O S D F T O Y E
V E A K Y N E N
E C I M Z S N P
C H I C A G O I
T R A I N M M T
```

Mama went to _____ to find work.

Ada Ruth stayed at home with_____.

Mama washed the _____.

Ada Ruth wrote her mama _____.

Under the Quilt of Night

By Deborah Hopkinson

Hopkinson, Deborah. *Under the Quilt of Night.* New York: Atheneum Books for Young Readers, 2001.

Objective: Students will listen to the story and research the role of quilts in the communication along the Underground Railroad.

AASL Standards

Information Literacy

Standard 1: The student who is information literate accesses information efficiently and effectively.

Standard 3: The student who is information literate uses information accurately and creatively.

Independent Learning

Standard 4: The student who is an independent learner is information literate and pursues information related to personal interests.

Skills

- Researching
- Fact and fiction

Grade Level: Third grade

Materials

- A collection of nonfiction books about the Underground Railroad
- Worksheet copied for each student

Step 1: Introduce the title, author, and illustrator. Read the first paragraph from the "A Note about the Story" in the back of the book. Tell the students this story combines facts and fiction. Explain: "We are going to find out what is fiction and what is fact in the story."

Step 2: Read the story and share the pictures. Talk about the events in the story. Some of the events could be true, and some could be false.

Step 3: Pass out worksheets. Under the title, write together as a class the events from the story.

Step 4: Tell students that they are going to read nonfiction information and determine which events in the story are fact and which are fiction about the Underground Railroad. Tell students that they will need to write the true facts from the resources on the right-hand side of the worksheet.

Step 5: Using the Web site http://pathways.thinkport.org and nonfiction books, have students complete the worksheet.

Closure: Share worksheets and talk about the fact and fiction parts of the story.

Other Resource

Under the Quilt of Night
By Deborah Hopkinson
New York: Atheneum Books for Young
Readers 2001

_____
_____
_____
_____
_____

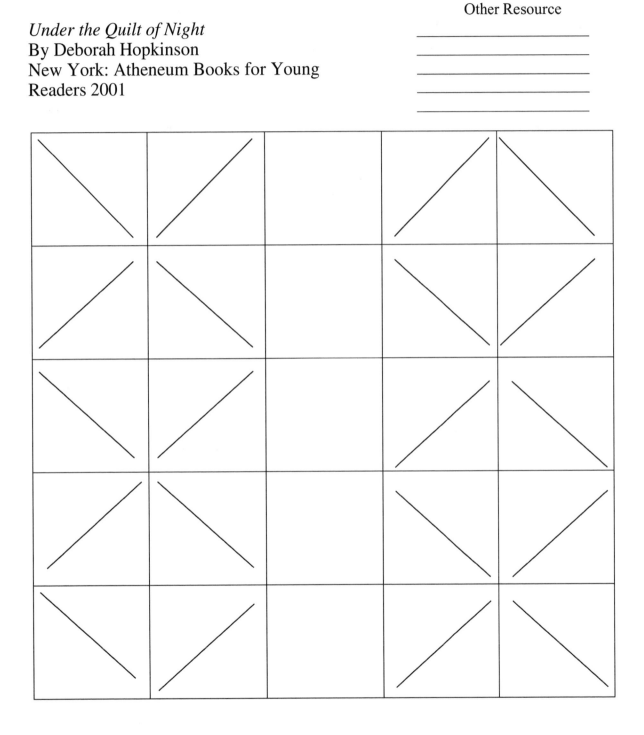

Resources for January

Kindergarten and First Grade

Brown, Marc. *Arthur and the Snow.* New York: Little, Brown and Company, 2005.

Ford, Bernette. *First Snow.* New York: Holiday House, 2005.

O'Malley, Kevin. *Straight to the Pole.* New York: Walker & Company, 2003.

Vestergaard, Hope. *Hello, Snow!* New York: Melanie Kroupa Books, 2004.

Second and Third Grade

Lester, Helen. *Tacky and the Winter Games.* New York: Houghton Mifflin, 2005.

Nagda, Ann Whitehead, and Cindy Bickel. *Polar Bear Math.* New York: Henry Holt, 2004.

Spinelli, Eileen. *Something to Tell the Grandcows.* Grand Rapids, MI: Eerdmans Books for Young Readers, 2004.

Hokey Pokey: Another Prickly Love Story

By Lisa Wheeler

Wheeler, Lisa. *Hokey Pokey: Another Prickly Love Story.* New York: Little, Brown and Company, 2006.

Objective: Students will listen to the story and dance the revised version of "The Hokey Pokey."

AASL Standard

Independent Learning

Standard 5: The student who is an independent learner is information literate and appreciates literature and other creative expressions of information.

Skills

- Library terms
- Reading enrichment

Grade Level: Kindergarten

Materials

- All students will either need the library book that they have selected for the week or a classroom book for the dance at the end of the lesson.

Step 1: Share the book cover, reading the title and author. Ask students if this title reminds them of anything. Ask them if they think this story has anything to do with the dance by the same title. Kindergarten students may not know this song, and you may have to sing or play the song. Give time for students to connect the story with personal experiences.

Step 2: Read the book and share the pictures.

Step 3: Review the following terms with the students: cover, spine, title, and author.

Step 4: Form a circle, and do the Hokey Pokey. First do the normal version with which they are familiar, then insert the parts of a book for the body parts.

Verse 1

Put the front of the book in,
Put the front of the book out,
Put the front of the book in and shake it all about.
You do the Hokey Pokey and turn yourself around and that's what it's all about.

Verse 2

    Put the back of the book in

Verse 3

    Put the spine of the book in

Verse 4

    Flash the title in

Verse 5

    Put the whole book in

Closure: Return to the circle and have students share their book titles with a partner. Call out book titles or types of books as the students get in line. Example: If you have a dog story, you may get in line.

Teacher's Notes:

If You'll Be My Valentine

By Cynthia Rylant

Rylant, Cynthia. *If You'll Be My Valentine.* New York: HarperCollins, 2005.

Objective: Students will listen to the story and match up the valentines with the one receiving the message. They will also write their own valentines and draw a picture clue to go along with the messages like the ones in the story text.

AASL Standards

Information Literacy

Standard 2: The student who is information literate evaluates information critically and competently.

Standard 3: The student who is information literate uses information accurately and creatively.

Skills

- Reading enrichment

Grade Level: First grade

Materials

- Ten sheets of paper
- Crayons
- Valentine fun sheet for each student
- Paper bag large enough to hold the valentines

Preparing the materials: Write or type out each of the valentines and draw the corresponding picture clue (see book). Laminate each and fold in half. Words should appear on the outside, and the picture clue should be on the inside of the folded half. Decorate the outside of the paper bag with hearts. Place the laminated valentines inside to use later in the lesson.

Step 1: Introduce the author of this story and stress that she is the same one who writes the Henry and Mudge books. Review where in the Everybody Section this book would be found using the call number on the spine to reinforce this concept.

Step 2: Read the story and share the pictures.

Step 3: Present the bag of valentines, and have a student draw out one at a time. Read the message and see if students can recall for whom that valentine was written. If needed, show the picture clue. Call on students until all the messages have been read.

Step 4: Move students to tables and give out the valentine fun sheet. Explain that the students will write a message for someone. They should fold the papers so that the message is on the outside and the picture clues appear on the inside.

Closure: Return to the story corner and give students time to read and share what they have written.

If you'll be my valentine

I'll_____

_____

_____

_____

_____

_____

_____

Sweet Hearts

By Jan Carr

Carr, Jan. *Sweet Hearts*. New York: Holiday House, 2003.

Objective: Students will listen to the story and understand that there are many different kinds of illustrations and will be able to identify each one.

AASL Standard

Information Literacy

Standard 3: The student who is information literate uses information accurately and creatively.

Skills

• Understanding and identifying illustrations

Grade Level: Second grade

Materials

• Word card pattern

• Card stock

• Books with different kinds of illustrations

Examples:
Collage

Carle, Eric. *The Very Hungry Caterpillar*. New York: Philomel Books, 1987.

Carr, Jan. *Sweet Hearts*. New York: Holiday House, 2003.

Watercolors

Park, W.B. *Who's Sick!* Boston: Houghton Mifflin, 1983.

Rylant, Cynthia. *All I See*. New York: Orchard Books, 1988.

Photos

Doering, Amanda. *Cats ABC: An Alphabet Book*. Mankato, MN: Capstone Press, 2005.

Hoban, Tana. *Count and See*. New York: Simon & Schuster Books for Young Readers, 1972.

Tempera Paint

Wheeler, Lisa. *Sailor Moo Cow at Sea*. New York: Atheneum Books for Young Readers, 2002.

Pencil

Wilder, Laura Ingalls. *Farmer Boy.* New York: HarperTrophy, 1933.

Woodcut

Martin, Jacqueline Briggs. *Snowflake Bentley.* Boston: Houghton Mifflin, 1998.

Step 1: Introduce the terms "title," "author," and "illustrator." Review the word illustration. Tell students that they will need to look carefully at the illustrations because you are going to talk about several different kinds of illustrations.

Step 2: Read the story, and share and discuss illustrations. Tell students that the illustrations in this book are called collage. The illustrator used paper cutouts to make the illustrations. Show word and definition cards for collage.

Step 3: Show examples of other kinds of illustrations and word and definition cards. Discuss with the students the difference and how to tell them apart.

Step 4: Show six books the students have not seen and see if they can identify the kind of illustration.

Closure: Allow time for students to share their favorite kind of illustration.

Teacher's Notes:

Pencil	Black drawings
Collage	Pieces of paper or other objects glued on paper.
Woodcut	Black outlines and colors inside
Watercolors	Light colors
Tempera Paint	Bright colors
Photos	Camera pictures

Happy Valentine's Day, Dolores

By Barbara Samuels

Samuels, Barbara. *Happy Valentine's Day, Dolores.* New York: Melanie Kroupa Books, 2006.

Objective: Students will listen to the story and understand the importance of giving credit for information used in a research project. Students will also identify all the parts of a print source.

AASL Standards

Social Responsibility

Standard 8: The student who contributes positively to the learning community and to society is information literate and practices ethical behavior in regard to information and information technology.

Standard 9: The student who contributes positively to the learning community and to society is information literate and participates effectively in groups to pursue and generate information.

Skills

- Identifying parts of a print source

Grade Level: Third grade

Materials

- Copy of a title and copyright page

- Worksheet for each student

- Six books with the title, author, publisher, and place of publication clearly visible on the title page

- A book with a bibliography

Preparing the materials: Make overheads of the title and copyright page. You can use a copy for educational purposes from a text for one year under the fair use policy.

Step 1: Introduce the title and author. Ask students if they have ever borrowed something from someone without permission.

Step 2: Read the story and share the pictures.

Step 3: Discuss using information for research and how we need to give credit for information we find in books, magazines, and on the Internet. Show students a book with a bibliography.

Step 4: Show the overheads of the title and the copyright pages and point out where to find the author, title, publisher, place of publication, and copyright date.

Step 5: Divide the class into six groups and give each group a preselected book. Give each student a worksheet and pencil. Explain the directions for the worksheet.

Step 6: Students complete worksheets.

Closure: Gather students back together and share and discuss their worksheets.

Match the words at the left with the examples at the right by drawing a line.

Publisher   Marc Brown

Place of Publication   Little, Brown & Company

Author   *D.W.'s Library Card*

Title   1999

Copyright Date   New York

Using your group's book and looking at the example, write a print source on the lines below.

Example: Samuels, Barbara. *Happy Valentine's Day, Dolores.* New York: Melanie Kroupa Books, 2006.

_____

_____

_____

_____

_____

_____

Resources for February

Kindergarten and First Grade

Bateman, Teresa. *Will You Be My Valenswine?* Morton Grove, IL: Whitman, 2005.

Cox, Judy. *Go to Sleep, Groundhog!* New York: Holiday House, 2004.

Cuyler, Margery. *Groundhog Stays Up Late.* New York: Walker & Company, 2005.

Haugen, Brenda. *The 100th Day of School.* Minneapolis, MN: Picture Window Books, 2004.

Ross, Tony. *Centipede's 100 Shoes.* New York: Henry Holt, 2003.

Spohn, Kate. *Turtle and Snake's Valentine's Day.* New York: Viking, 2003.

Wallace, Nancy Elizabeth. *The Valentine Express.* New York: Marshall Cavendish, 2004.

Wells, Rosemary. *Emily's First 100 Days of School.* New York: Scholastic, 2000.

Second and Third Grade

Bader, Bonnie. *100 Monsters in My School.* New York: Grosset & Dunlap, 2002.

Cuyler, Margery. *100th Day Worries.* New York: Simon & Schuster Books for Young Readers, 2000.

Harris, Trudy. *100 Days of School.* Brookfield, CT: Millbrook Press, 1999.

Old, Wendie. *The Groundhog Day Book of Facts and Fun.* Morton Grove, IL: Whitman, 2004.

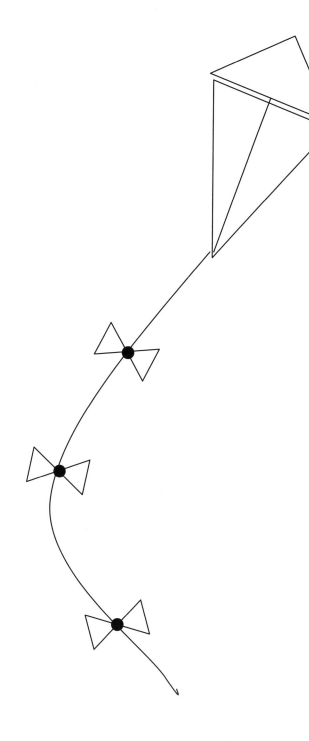

March

If You Give a Pig a Party

By Laura Numeroff

Numeroff, Laura. *If You Give a Pig a Party*. New York: Laura Geringer Books, 2005.

Objective: Students will listen to the story, sing Happy Birthday to Dr. Seuss, look for his books on the library online catalog, and then locate them on the shelf.

AASL Standards

Information Literacy

Standard 1: The student who is information literate accesses information efficiently and effectively.
Standard 2: The student who is information literate evaluates information critically and competently.
Standard 3: The student who is information literate uses information accurately and creatively.

Skills

- Reading enrichment

- Author recognition

- Introduction to online catalog

Grade Level: Kindergarten

Materials

- Party hats for each child

- Overhead or copy printed on paper

- LCD projector

Preparing the materials: If possible, set up the LCD projector so that you can project the listing of Dr. Seuss books on a big screen. If this is not possible, copy the listing from your online catalog program and make it into an overhead. Set up equipment ahead of class time. Either create the supplied overhead page or copy it onto paper.

Step 1: Give out the party hats so that each student has one to wear. Introduce the lesson by explaining that we are having a birthday party for Dr. Seuss, one of our favorite authors. His birthday is always the first week in March, and schools all over America do special activities in honor of this special person. Show the book and share the title. Make the connection that this is a book about a pig planning a party. This story was not written by Dr. Seuss, but we will find some of his books during our activity time. How many students like birthday parties? Does anyone in this class have a March birthday like Dr. Seuss? Give time for student interaction. What do you do to celebrate at your house?

Step 2: Read the story and share the pictures. Discuss what things the mouse wants to do in order to have a birthday party.

Step 3: Sing Happy Birthday to Dr. Seuss.

Step 4: Stress that here in the library, students can look up all of Dr. Seuss's books on the online catalog program. Move students so that you either show the list on a big screen or overhead. Use this time to introduce the idea that we cannot keep all of the titles of our library books in our head, so the computer keeps track of all the information. Explain that if we type in our favorite author, the computer quickly does all the work, and then gives us a list.

Step 5: Bring up the listing and show the students how many books written by Dr. Seuss you have in the library. Record that number either on the overhead or on your paper copy.

Step 6: Show the call number of the Dr. Seuss books and then move students to the shelf where they are located.

Closure: Pull some favorites off the shelf and see if students can read the titles. Check to see if Dr. Seuss is listed as the author. Collect books for them to read back in the classroom.

Teacher's Notes:

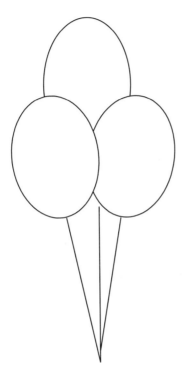

We have_____ Dr. Seuss books in our library.

Minnie and Moo:
The Case of the Missing Jelly Donut

By Denys Cazet

Cazet, Denys. *Minnie and Moo: The Case of the Missing Jelly Donut.* New York: HarperCollins, 2005.

Objective: Students will listen to the story, understand that authors write books in a series, and, with the help from the librarian, search the online catalog and locate authors' books.

AASL Standards

Information Literacy

Standard 1: The student who is information literate accesses information efficiently and effectively.

Standard 2: The student who is information literate evaluates information critically and competently.

Standard 3: The student who is information literate uses information accurately and creatively.

Skills

- Understand the term "series"
- Search for authors using the online catalog

Grade Level: First grade

Materials

- Worksheet for each student
- Computers logged onto the online catalog
- Several other books in the same series

Preparing the materials: Copy the worksheet for each student or just make enough for one class and laminate. The worksheets will last longer because students are not writing on them.

Step 1: Introduce title and author. Read story and share pictures.

Step 2: Show other titles in this same series. Tell students that the main characters will be the same in all the books.

Step 3: Gather students at the computers and pass out the worksheets.

Step 4: Assist students as they type in the authors' names.

Step 5: When the list of books appears, show students the title, author, and call number. If the author has written several books, there may be more than one page of books. Show students how to access the other pages.

Closure: Look for books on the shelves using the worksheet.

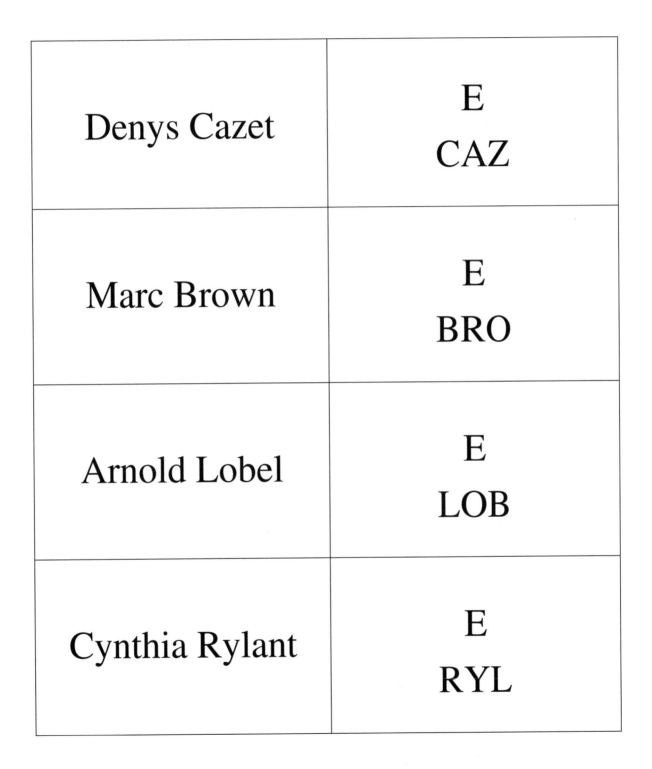

Denys Cazet	E CAZ
Marc Brown	E BRO
Arnold Lobel	E LOB
Cynthia Rylant	E RYL

A Frog in the Bog

By Karma Wilson

Wilson, Karma. *A Frog in the Bog*. New York: Margaret K. McElderry Books, 2003.

Objective: Students will listen to the story and identify the style of writing that the story represents. Students will also search by title and subject on the online catalog.

AASL Standards

Information Literacy

Standard 1: The student who is information literate accesses information efficiently and effectively.

Standard 2: The student who is information literate evaluates information critically and competently.

Standard 3: The student who is information literate uses information accurately and creatively.

Skills

- Introduction to writing styles: standard, rhyming, and alliteration
- Searching the online catalog

Grade Level: Second grade

Materials

- Computers
- Worksheet and pencils for each student
- Word and definition cards

Step 1: Introduce the three styles of writing. Show word cards, definition cards, and examples.

Step 2: Introduce the title and author of the book *A Frog in the Bog*. Tell students to listen closely to the words and be ready to share what kind of style of writing is used.

Step 3: Read the story and share pictures.

Step 4: Ask students what style of writing this story represents. Students share their favorite rhyme from the story.

Step 5: Help students identify the one alliteration phrase in this story (a little bit bigger).

Step 6: Move students to the computers. Have students share computers if you do not have one computer for each student. Pass out worksheets and pencils.

Step 7: Open the online catalog and guide students through the process of searching for the subject "rhyming books" and titles that are examples of alliteration (examples: Patty's Pumpkin Patch; Slinky, Scaly, Slithery Snakes; Flashy, Fantastic Rainforest Frogs; and Four Freckled Frogs).

Step 8: Students select a book from the examples and try to find the book on the shelf using the call number and title. Have the students use the worksheet to record the title and call number before searching the shelves.

Title:_____

Call Number:_____

- -

Title:_____

Call Number:_____

Standard	Regular text without rhyming
Rhyming	Words that have the same ending sounds
Alliteration	Words that begin with the same letter

The dog was brown and white.

A dog sat with a frog on a log.

Bowman Braves beat Beavercreek Beavers.

The Giant and the Beanstalk

By Diane Stanley

Stanley, Diane. *The Giant and the Beanstalk.* New York: HarperCollins, 2004.

Objective: Students will listen to the story and look for fairy-tale books in the library.

AASL Standards

Information Literacy

Standard 1: The student who is information literate accesses information efficiently and effectively.

Standard 2: The student who is information literate evaluates information critically and competently.

Standard 3: The student who is information literate uses information accurately and creatively.

Skills

- Reading enrichment
- Fairy-tale genre
- Text-to-text comparison

Grade Level: Second grade

Materials

- Worksheet for each student
- Overhead

Step 1: Using the overhead, introduce the students to the 398.2 section of the nonfiction area of the library. Explain that Mr. Dewey grouped all of the folktales and fairy-tale books under the same number so that they would be easier to find. Also explain that these books are not true. That is always confusing to students.

Step 2: Share the title and author of this story. This story ties nicely into other nursery rhymes with the main character Jack, for example, "Jack and Jill." Ask students to listen for all of the "Jacks" in the story as you read and share the pictures.

Step 3: Lead the students in a discussion of all of the Jacks mentioned in the text. Make a list on the board and help students recall the wording of the nursery rhymes. They are listed in the back of the text so teachers can have a student read them if needed. Visit the 398.2 section and book talk several fairy tales in your collection.

Step 4: Move the class to the computers, and lead the students through the process of accessing the card catalog and doing a subject search for fairy tales. Pair up students and give each one a half sheet of the worksheet to record his or her fairy-tale selection. Students will record the title, author, and call number. If students have time, they can go back to the 398.2 section and locate the book.

Optional Activity: Have students compare this story of Jack with the traditional version. It will make a good compare-and-contrast lesson by itself. The ending is completely different, and the students will enjoy this twisted, giant-friendly tale.

Fairy Tales

398.2

Fairy Tales

Title_____

Author_____

Call Number_____

- -

Fairy Tales

Title_____

Author_____

Call Number_____

The Mystery of Eatum Hall

By John Kelly and Cathy Tincknell

Kelly, John, and Cathy Tincknell. *The Mystery of Eatum Hall.* Cambridge, MA: Candlewick Press, 2004.

Objective: Students will listen to the story, look for mystery books on the library online catalog, and then locate them on the shelf.

AASL Standards

Information Literacy

Standard 1: The student who is information literate accesses information efficiently and effectively.

Standard 2: The student who is information literate evaluates information critically and competently.

Standard 3: The student who is information literate uses information accurately and creatively.

Skills

- Reading enrichment

- Mystery genre

Grade Level: Third grade

Materials

- Worksheet for each student

Step 1: Share the front of the cover and read the title. Brainstorm what mysteries are, and write a definition on the board.

Step 2: Ask the students to listen for what the mystery is in the story and how it gets solved. Read the story, and share the pictures.

Step 3: Spend time discussing the mystery and solution with the students. At what point in the story did the reader catch on to the wolf's extreme measures to trap his guest who came to his house party? How did the illustrator help with picture clues? Does our definition of mysteries support calling this book a mystery? Do we need to change our definition?

Closure: Go over the directions for the worksheet, and model accessing the online catalog for your students. Writing the steps on the board will help minimize problems for students. If you have a limited number of computers, pair students with partners. Provide similar picture book mysteries for silent reading time while students are waiting their turn at the computer.

Access the online catalog system, do a subject search for mysteries, and answer the following questions.

Number of mysteries in our library_____

Title of a mystery_____

Author_____

Illustrator_____

Call number_____

Publisher_____

Place of publication_____

Number of pages in this book_____

Copyright date_____

Summarize the story

_____

_____

_____

_____

Find this book on the shelf, and show your librarian.

Resources for March

Kindergarten and First Grade

Adler, David A. *Bones and the Big Yellow Mystery.* New York: Viking, 2004.

Stanley, Diane. *Goldie and the Three Bears.* New York: HarperCollins, 2003.

Wood, Audrey. *Alphabet Mystery.* New York: Blue Sky, 2003.

Second and Third Grade

Cushman, Doug. *Inspector Hopper.* New York: HarperCollins, 2000.

Cushman, Doug. *Inspector Hopper's Mystery Year.* New York: HarperCollins, 2003.

Krull, Kathleen. *The Boy on Fairfield Street.* New York: Random House, 2004.

Pallotta, Jerry. *The Beetle Alphabet Book.* Watertown, MA: Charlesbridge, 2004.

Woods, Mae. *Dr. Seuss.* Edina, MN: Abdo, 2000.

April

Really Rabbits

By Virginia Kroll

Kroll, Virginia. *Really Rabbits*. Watertown, MA: Charlesbridge, 2006.

Objective: Students will listen to the story and realize that information can be collected from various sources.

AASL Standards

Information Literacy

Standard 1: The student who is information literate accesses information efficiently and effectively.

Standard 2: The student who is information literate evaluates information critically and competently.

Standard 3: The student who is information literate uses information accurately and creatively.

Skills

- Author recognition
- Retelling
- Technology

Grade Level: Kindergarten

Materials

- Stuffed rabbit
- An easy biography of an author that the students will recognize (example: Woods, Mae. *Dr. Seuss*. Edina, MN, Adbo, 2000).

Step 1: Using the front of the book, read the title and author. Write the author's name on the board. Ask students to explain what an author does. Read the story and share the pictures.

Step 2: As the students pass the rabbit around, they each take a turn in retelling part of the story. The teacher needs to guide this process so that students tell the events in order.

Step 3: Show the author biography that you have pulled ahead of time. Have several to share if your collection has more available. Point out to students that sometimes we can learn about an author by looking up information in a book. Show pages and pictures so that students become familiar with the concept that this is a fact book about a famous person. Not all authors have a book written about them, but sometimes information about an author is posted on a Web site.

Closure: Group the kindergarten class around a computer and access the following Web site: www.hachettebookgroupusa.com/authors/65/857. Read to the class the short biographical sketch. Return to the circle and make a list of facts about Virginia Kroll that students learned from the Web site.

In the Garden: Who's Been Here?

By Lindsay Barrett George

George, Lindsay Barrett. *In the Garden: Who's Been Here?* New York: Greenwillow Books, 2006.

Objective: Students will listen to the story, sequence the story, and look up bugs on the Internet.

AASL Standards

Independent Learning

Standard 6: The student who is an independent learner is information literate and strives for excellence in information seeking and knowledge generation.

Social Responsibility

Standard 8: The student who contributes positively to the learning community and to society is information literate and practices ethical behavior in regard to information and information technology.

Skills

- Sequencing
- Technology

Grade Level: First grade

Materials

- Worksheet for each student
- Eight large caterpillars cut from green paper (see pattern, or use a die cut machine)
- Venn diagram enlarged on board

Preparing the materials: List the following on the green caterpillars: chipmunk, worm, rabbit, slug, crow, mouse, woodchuck, and mole.

Step 1: Share the front of the cover and read the title. Brainstorm what could be hiding in the garden. Make a list of animals and insects that the students come up with before hearing the story.

Step 2: Students should listen for the animals and insects hiding in the story. Read the story and share the pictures.

Step 3: Make a new list of items that were in the story, and compare it with the first list. Using the Venn diagram, place the items in the appropriate circles. Were their predictions correct? Using the caterpillars, let the class sequence the animals and insects as they appeared in the garden.

Closure: Access the following Web site ahead of time for your students and go over the directions for the worksheet: www.whatsthatbug.com. Write the Web site on the board, and have the students record the Web site on the line at the bottom of the worksheet. Talk about who researched and found the information on the Web site. Tell students we need to give credit to the author of information they found when researching. If you have a limited number of computers, pair students with partners. Provide garden and insect books for silent reading time while students are waiting their turn at the computer. You could use older students from other classes to help students read the information on the Web site.

Teacher's Notes:

Venn Diagram

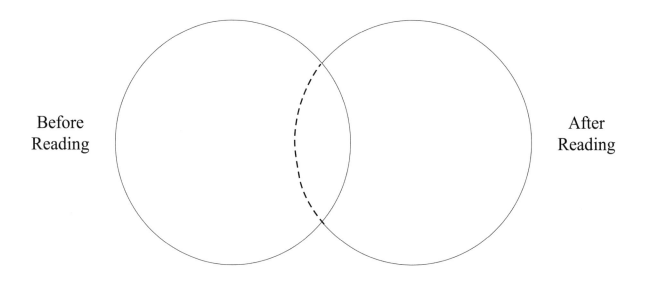

Before
Reading

After
Reading

Pattern for Caterpillar

 **Bugs**

What bug is in your garden?

Scroll down through the bugs on the Web site. Pick your favorite and answer the following questions.

Name of bug_____

Describe your bug.	Draw your bug.
_____	
_____	
_____	
_____	
_____	
_____	
_____	
_____	
_____	
_____	
_____	
_____	

I found my information on the Web site:_____

The author of this Web site is:_____

Farfallina & Marcel

By Holly Keller

Keller, Holly. *Farfallina & Marcel.* New York: Greenwillow Books, 2002.

Objective: Students will listen to the story, predict what will happen in the middle of the story, access a butterfly Web site, and draw and label the life cycle of Farfallina, the main character in the story.

AASL Standard

Social Responsibility

Standard 8: The student who contributes positively to the learning community and to society is information literate and practices ethical behavior in regard to information and information technology.

Skills

- Making predictions
- Finding information on a Web site
- Bookmarking a Web site for later use

Grade Level: Second grade

Materials

- Computers logged onto the Internet
- Worksheet and pencils for each student

Step 1: Introduce the title, author, and call number. Discuss the call number and identify the kind of book. Tell students that this book has a few real facts in it, even though it is an easy fiction book.

Step 2: Read the story, share pictures, and discuss the real facts in the story (examples: caterpillars rest in a cocoon, butterflies fly south for the winter, etc.). Write facts on the board.

Step 3: Gather students at the computers, pass out worksheets, and tell students they are going to check the facts and draw and label Farfallina's life cycle.

Step 4: Help students type in the Web site www.enchantedlearning.com/subjects/butterfly/. Then have them mark it in their favorites.

Step 5: To check the facts, select "All about butterflies" on the left of the screen. Scroll down to see all the facts. Discuss the facts about butterflies. Find who wrote the information for the Web site, and record the author on the worksheet.

Step 6: In the same location, find the four cycles of a butterfly, and complete the worksheet by drawing a picture of each cycle and writing the name of the cycle in the appropriate quarter of the circle.

Closure: Share worksheets.

Life Cycle of Farfallina
www.enchantedlearning.com/subjects/butterfly/

Author of Web site_____

Name_____

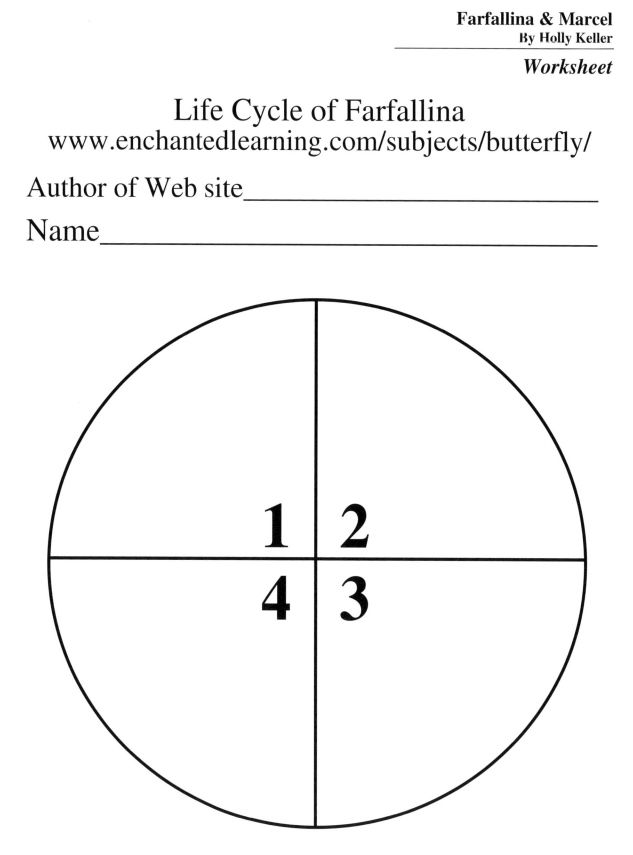

Diary of a Spider

By Doreen Cronin

Cronin, Doreen. *Diary of a Spider.* New York: Joanna Cotler Books, 2005.

Lesson 1

Objective: Students will listen to the story and record real facts about spiders.

AASL Standards

Information Literacy

Standard 2: The student who is information literate evaluates information critically and competently.

Standard 3: The student who is information literate uses information accurately and creatively.

Independent Learning

Standard 6: The student who is an independent learner is information literate and strives for excellence in information seeking and knowledge generation.

Skills

• Gathering information

Grade Level: Third grade

Materials

• Worksheet for each student

• Pencils

Step 1: Pass out worksheets and pencils. Introduce the terms "title," "author," and "illustrator." Tell the students that they need to listen to the story and record facts on their worksheet. Even though this story is a fiction book, there are real facts about spiders.

Step 2: Read story and share pictures.

Step 3: Students share and discuss facts.

Closure: Discuss how to check the accuracy of the facts the students have gathered. Students should respond with "using nonfiction books or the Internet to check for accurate facts." Tell students in their next lesson, you will check the Internet for accuracy.

Lesson 2

Objective: Students will search for a spider Web site using a search engine and check for accuracy of the facts from the first lesson.

AASL Standard

Social Responsibility

Standard 8: The student who contributes positively to the learning community and to society is information literate and practices ethical behavior in regard to information and information technology.

Skills

- Using a search engine
- Gathering information

Grade Level: Third grade

Materials

- Computers logged onto the Internet
- Worksheets from Lesson 1
- Pencils

Step 1: Review worksheet from first lesson.

Step 2: Have students click on the current Web address and type in a search engine. Examples: www.yahooilgans.com; www.awesomelibrary.org/ An example of a useful Web site on spiders is: www.tooter4kids.com/Spiders/Spiders.htm

Step 3: Direct students to type in "spiders" and click on "search."

Step 4: Help students decide on the best Web site to select by reading the description. Remind students to write down the Web site to give credit to the person or persons who created the Web site.

Step 5: After selecting a Web site, students will complete the worksheet.

Closure: Gather students and share worksheets.

Teacher's Notes:

Lesson 1

Facts about Spiders

Diary of a Spider   **Web Resource**_____

1._____   1._____

2._____   2._____

3._____   3._____

4._____   4._____

5._____   5._____

6._____   6._____

7._____   7._____

8._____   8._____

9._____   9._____

10._____   10._____

Resources for April

Kindergarten and First Grade

Cain, Sheridan. *The Crunching Munching Caterpillar.* Wilton, CT: Tiger Tales, 2000.

Edwards, Pamela Duncan. *Clara Caterpillar.* New York: HarperCollins, 2001.

George, Lindsay Barrett. *The Secret.* New York: Greenwillow Books, 2005.

Ross, Michael Elsohn. *Snug as a Bug.* San Francisco, CA: Chronicle, 2004.

Spinelli, Eileen. *In Our Backyard Garden.* New York: Simon & Schuster Books for Young Readers, 2004.

Second and Third Grade

Hopkinson, Deborah. *A Packet of Seeds.* New York: Greenwillow Books, 2004.

Robbins, Ken. *Seeds.* New York: Atheneum Books for Young Readers, 2005.

May

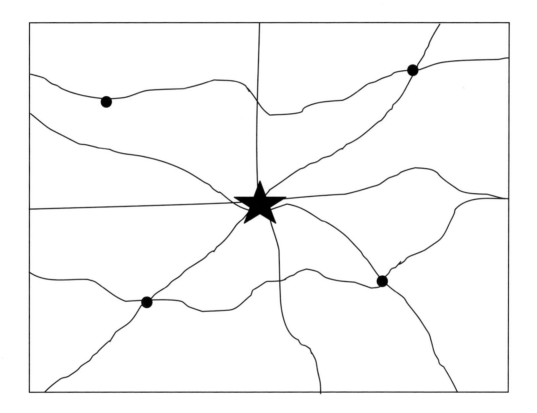

Bedtime in the Southwest

By Mona Hodgson

Hodgson, Mona. *Bedtime in the Southwest.* Flagstaff, AZ: Rising Moon, 2004.

Objective: Students will listen to the story, match up the word cards with the animal pictures, and look up desert animals on the Web site.

AASL Standard

Independent Learning

Standard 6: The student who is an independent learner is information literate and strives for excellence in information seeking and knowledge generation.

Skills

- Word recognition
- Technology
- Compare and contrast

Grade Level: Kindergarten

Materials

- Eleven colorful pieces of construction paper
- Children's atlas

Preparing the materials: Write the following animal names on the construction paper, one name to each of the 11 sheets. Animals: roadrunner, lizard, coyote, porcupine, owl, rabbit, bird, skunk, crow, rat, and pronghorn.

Step 1: Using the children's atlas, show the students the southwest part of the United States where the desert region would be located. Explain that this is the setting for this story. Talk about what we mean by "setting." Write the word "setting" on the board. Is this desert different from where you live? Have the students look at the cover of the book for picture clues as to what the desert might be like. Share pictures from the atlas or use another book from your library that might have better pictures.

Step 2: Students should listen for discussion of the animals in the story and see if they recognize any that live in their state.

Step 3: Compare the desert to where they live and make a list of things that would be different (keep these simple, such as hot, dry, etc.).

Step 4: Match the names of the animals on the word cards with the pictures in the book. Lay the word cards out and help students read the names. Taking one picture at a time, let the students match up the picture with the correct name. Help with the ones that are more difficult to identify.

Closure: Access the following Web site ahead of time for your students: www.desertusa. com/animal.html. Show them how to click on the picture of the animals to get more information. Locate one or two of the animals that were mentioned in the story.

Animal Strike at the Zoo It's True!

By Karma Wilson

Wilson, Karma. *Animal Strike at the Zoo It's True!* New York: HarperCollins, 2006.

Objective: Students will listen to the story, look up zoo animals, and then play the "I'm going to the zoo" game.

AASL Standards

Independent Learning

Standard 6: The student who is an independent learner is information literate and strives for excellence in information seeking and knowledge generation.

Social Responsibility

Standard 7: The student who contributes positively to the learning community and to society is information literate and recognizes the importance of information to a democratic society.

Skills

- Technology

Grade Level: First grade

Materials

- Worksheet for each student

Step 1: Ask the students if any of them have been to the zoo. Give time to share stories and special moments. Read the title of the book and ask if anyone has a clue as to what we mean by a "strike." Make a list of student predictions for the end of the story.

Step 2: Read the book and share the pictures. Check the predictions that were recorded at the beginning of the story.

Step 3: Explain how, by using the Internet, we can visit the national zoo located in Washington, D.C. Group the students around your computers and access the following Web site: www.nationalzoo.si.edu. Show students how they can bring up more information by clicking with the mouse on any of the animal pictures. Select students to click on different animals.

Step 4: Students should return to tables and complete the worksheet. Go over the directions and give out supplies.

Closure: After finishing the worksheet, students return to the circle and play "I'm going to the zoo."

Game: First student holds up a picture and says, "I'm going to the zoo, and I plan to see a _____." Each student after that must remember what the person in front of them said. The students each hold up their picture and add the animal that they have drawn to the statement. Proceed around the circle as time allows.

- -

What animal would you like to see at the zoo? Write the name of the animal on the line, and then draw a picture to illustrate your visit.

- -

I'm going to the zoo, and I plan to see a

_____.

Last Day Blues

By Julie Danneberg

Danneberg, Julie. *Last Day Blues.* Watertown, MA: Charlesbridge, 2006.

Lesson 1

Objective: Students will listen to the story and brainstorm ideas for local summer activities. Students will then research these ideas and make advertising posters for these activities.

AASL Standards

Independent Learning

Standard 6: The student who is an independent learner is information literate and strives for excellence in information seeking and knowledge generation.

Social Responsibility

Standard 7: The student who contributes positively to the learning community and to society is information literate and recognizes the importance of information to a democratic society.

Standard 8: The student who contributes positively to the learning community and to society is information literate and practices ethical behavior in regard to information and information technology.

Standard 9: The student who contributes positively to the learning community and to society is information literate and participates effectively in groups to pursue and generate information.

Skills
- Researching
- Collaborating

Grade Level: Second grade

Materials
- Scrap paper and pencils
- Large poster board
- Markers

Step 1: Introduce the title, author, and illustrator. Discuss the title, *Last Day Blues,* and the fact that the title relates to the last day of school and that "blues" means to fell sad.

Step 2: Read the story and share the pictures.

Step 3: Record on the board things the students in the story will miss about school and also the things your students will miss.

Step 4: Discuss fun activities your students can participate in locally during the summer. Examples: YMCA programs, baseball and softball leagues, ride bike trail, explore the city, recreation, and so on.

Closure: Discuss ways to find out more information about these activities. Examples: Internet, phone calls, writing letters, and so on.

Lesson 2

Objective: Students will collaborate with their classmates by researching a summer activity and making an advertising poster for their activity.

AASL Standards

Independent Learning

Standard 6: The student who is an independent learner is information literate and strives for excellence in information seeking and knowledge generation.

Social Responsibility

Standard 7: The student who contributes positively to the learning community and to society is information literate and recognizes the importance of information to a democratic society.

Standard 8: The student who contributes positively to the learning community and to society is information literate and practices ethical behavior in regard to information and information technology.

Standard 9: The student who contributes positively to the learning community and to society is information literate and participates effectively in groups to pursue and generate information.

Skills

- Collaborating
- Researching

Grade Level: Second grade

Materials

- Worksheet for each group
- Pencils
- Large poster paper
- Markers and crayons

Step 1: Divide the class into groups depending on how many activities you selected to research.

Step 2: Allow students to choose the activity they would like to research.

Step 3: Each group will research its activity using the Internet. If the activity is not on the Internet, then students can use the phone or e-mail to gather information.

Step 4: You will need to research ahead of time so that you can guide students to the proper resources.

Step 5: Each group will complete a worksheet on the activity and create an advertising poster to hang in the halls.

Closure: Hang posters in the halls for all to share and view.

Lesson 2

Activity:_____

Cost:_____

Dates and Times:_____

Location:_____

Materials Needed:_____

_____

_____

_____

Resources:_____

_____

_____

_____

Students in group:_____

The Big Trip

By Valeri Gorbachev

Gorbachev, Valeri. *The Big Trip.* New York: Philomel, 2004.

Objective: Students will listen to the story, brainstorm ideas for exciting trips, and research different modes of transportation to arrive at the locations.

AASL Standards

Independent Learning

Standard 6: The student who is an independent learner is information literate and strives for excellence in information seeking and knowledge generation.

Social Responsibility

Standard 7: The student who contributes positively to the learning community and to society is information literate and recognizes the importance of information to a democratic society.

Standard 9: The student who contributes positively to the learning community and to society is information literate and participates effectively in groups to pursue and generate information.

Skills

- Story elements
- Researching
- Searching the Internet

Grade Level: Third grade

Materials

- Worksheet for each group
- Pencils

Step 1: Introduce the title and author. Discuss the front cover, with Pig hanging out of a hot air balloon with a map. Allow time for students to share trips they have taken or would like to take.

Step 2: Read the story and share the pictures. Discuss the characters, Pig and Goat, the ideas of setting, problem, and solution.

Step 3: Brainstorm ideas for trips this summer. Write the responses on the board. Tell students they will need to know the city and state of the trip. Example: Disney World, Orlando, Florida.

Step 4: Divide the students into groups, four or five students per group. Give each group a worksheet and pencil.

Step 5: Explain to the students that they are going to research their trip using Web sites. They will be researching how far in miles and time and also how much the trip would cost by air, train, bus, and car. Depending on the makeup of your class and your time frame, you might modify this activity and have each group only research one mode of transportation.

Step 6: Gather students at the computers and search each of the Web sites for a destination as an example for the class. Example: Your town and state to Ames, Iowa.

Step 7: Allow time for students to complete worksheets.

   Closure: Share worksheets and information.

   Teacher's Notes:

Worksheet

Use the Web sites to answer the questions about your destination.

Names of students in your group:_____

_____

What is your destination?_____

Car: www.mapquest.com

How long would your trip last in hours and minutes?_____

How long would your trip be in miles?_____

How much gas would you need if your car averaged 20 miles per gallon?
_____

How much money would you need if the gas is $3.00 per gallon?
_____

Bus: www.greyhound.com

How long would your trip last in hours and minutes?_____

How much would your trip cost?_____

Plane: www.delta.com

How long would your trip last in hours and minutes?_____

How much would your trip cost?_____

Train: www.amtrak.com

How long would your trip last in hours and minutes?_____

How much would your trip cost?_____

Resources for May

Kindergarten and First Grade

Slate, Joseph. *Miss Bindergarten Takes a Field Trip with Kindergarten.* New York: Dutton Children's Books, 2001.

Winthrop, Elizabeth. *Dancing Granny.* Tarrytown, NY: Marshall Cavendish, 2003.

Second and Third Grade

dePaola, Tomie. *Strega Nona Takes a Vacation.* New York: Putnam, 2000.

Hobbs, Leigh. *Old Tom's Holiday.* Atlanta, GA: Peachtree, 2004.

Pattison, Darcy. *The Journey of Oliver K. Woodman.* New York: Harcourt, 2003.

Appendix

Information Literacy

Standard 1

Curious George Visits the Library
The Firefighters' Thanksgiving
The First Day of Winter
A Frog in the Bog
The Giant and the Beanstalk
The Hello, Goodbye Window
I.Q. Goes to the Library
I Wish Santa Would Come By Helicopter
If You Give a Pig a Party
Jeepers Creepers
Minnie and Moo: The Case of the Missing Jelly Donut
The Mystery of Eatum Hall
Mr. Wiggle's Book
One Witch
An Orange for Frankie
Really Rabbits
Skeleton Hiccups
Ten Little Mummies
Thank You, Thanksgiving
The Three Bears' Christmas
Under the Quilt of Night
Wild about Books

Standard 2

All You Need for a Snowman
Coming on Home Soon
Diary of a Spider
A Frog in the Bog
The Giant and the Beanstalk
The Hello, Goodbye Window
If You Give a Pig a Party
If You'll Be My Valentine
Minnie and Moo: The Case of the Missing Jelly Donut
The Mystery of Eatum Hall
Really Rabbits

Standard 3

All You Need for a Snowman
Coming on Home Soon
Diary of a Spider

The First Day of Winter
A Frog in the Bog
The Giant and the Beanstalk
I Wish Santa Would Come by Helicopter
If You Give a Pig a Party
If You'll Be My Valentine
Minnie and Moo: The Case of the Missing Jelly Donut
The Mystery of Eatum Hall
An Orange for Frankie
Really Rabbits
Snowmen at Christmas
Sweet Hearts
That's Our Librarian
The Three Bears' Christmas
Turkey Surprise
Under the Quilt of Night
Why Is It Snowing?

Independent Learning

Standard 4

An Orange for Frankie
That's Our Librarian
Under the Quilt of Night

Standard 5

Hokey Pokey: Another Prickly Love Story
Turkey Surprise

Standard 6

Animal Strike at the Zoo It's True!
Bedtime in the Southwest
The Big Trip
Diary of a Spider
In the Garden: Who's Been Here?
Last Day Blues

Social Responsibility

Standard 7

Animal Strike at the Zoo It's True!
The Big Trip
Happy Valentine's Day, Dolores
Last Day Blues
Rosa

Standard 8

Diary of a Spider
Farfallina & Marcel
Last Day Blues

Standard 9

Happy Valentine's Day, Dolores
Last Day Blues

Bibliography

Adler, David A. *Bones and the Big Yellow Mystery.* New York: Viking, 2004.

Allen, Susan, and Jane Lindaman. *Read Anything Good Lately.* Minneapolis, MN: Millbrook Press, 2003.

Appelt, Kathi. *Merry Christmas, Merry Crow.* New York: Harcourt, 2005.

Archer, Peggy. *Turkey Surprise.* New York: Dial Books for Young Readers, 2005.

Atwell, Debby. *The Thanksgiving Door.* Boston: Houghton Mifflin, 2003.

Aylesworth, Jim. *Naughty Little Monkeys.* New York: Dutton Children's Books, 2003.

Bader, Bonnie. *100 Monsters in My School.* New York: Grosset & Dunlap, 2002.

Bateman, Teresa. *Will You Be My Valenswine?* Morton Grove, IL: Whitman, 2005.

Bauld, Jane Scoggins. *We Need Principals.* Mankato, MN: Pebble Books, 2000.

Boelts, Maribeth. *The Firefighters' Thanksgiving.* New York: G.P. Putnam's Sons, 2004.

Bond, Rebecca. *A City Christmas Tree.* New York: Little, Brown and Company, 2005.

Brett, Jan. *Who's That Knocking on Christmas Eve?* New York: Putnam, 2002.

Brown, Marc. *Arthur and the Snow.* New York: Little, Brown and Company, 2005.

Brown, Marc. *D.W.'s Library Card.* Boston: Little, Brown and Company, 2001.

Bruss, Deborah. *Book! Book! Book!* New York: Arthur A. Levine Books, 2001.

Buehner, Caralyn. *Snowmen At Christmas.* New York: Dial Books for Young Readers, 2005.

Bullard, Lisa. *Trick-or-Treat on Milton Street.* Minneapolis, MN: Carolrhoda Books, 2001.

Cain, Sheridan. *The Crunching Munching Caterpillar.* Wilton, CT: Tiger Tales, 2000.

Carle, Eric. *The Very Hungry Caterpillar.* New York: Philomel Books, 1987.

Carr, Jan. *Sweet Hearts.* New York: Holiday House, 2003.

Cazet, Denys. *Minnie and Moo: The Case of the Missing Jelly Donut.* New York: HarperCollins, 2005.

Chocolate, Deborah M. Newton. *My First Kwanzaa Book.* New York: Scholastic, 1999.

Climo, Shirley. *Cobweb Christmas.* New York: HarperCollins, 2001.

Colfer, Eoin. *The Legend of Spud Murphy.* New York: Hyperion Books for Children, 2004.

Cousins, Lucy. *Maisy Goes to the Library.* Cambridge, MA: Candlewick Press, 2005.

Cox, Judy. *Go to Sleep, Groundhog!* New York: Holiday House, 2004.

Craig, Paula, and Carol Thompson. *Mr. Wiggle's Book.* Columbus, OH: Waterbird Books, 2004.

Cronin, Doreen. *Diary of a Spider.* New York: Joanna Cotler Books, 2005.

Cushman, Doug. *Inspector Hopper.* New York: HarperCollins, 2000.

Cushman, Doug. *Inspector Hopper's Mystery Year.* New York: HarperCollins, 2003.

Cuyler, Margery. *100th Day Worries.* New York: Simon & Schuster Books for Young Readers, 2000.

Cuyler, Margery. *Groundhog Stays Up Late.* New York: Walker & Company, 2005.

Cuyler, Margery. *Skeleton Hiccups.* New York: Margaret K. McElderry. 2002.

Dahl, Michael. *Eggs and Legs: Counting by Twos.* Minneapolis, MN: Picture Window Books, 2005.

Danneberg, Julie. *Last Day Blues.* Watertown, MA: Charlesbridge, 2006.

dePaola, Tomie. *Strega Nona Takes a Vacation.* New York: Putnam, 2000.

Doering, Amanda. *Cats ABC: An Alphabet Book.* Mankato, MN: Capstone Press, 2002.

Duval, Kathy. *The Three Bears' Christmas.* New York: Holiday House, 2005.

Edwards, Pamela Duncan. *Clara Caterpillar.* New York: HarperCollins, 2001.

Ellis, Rowland-Grey, and Teddy Kentor. *The Scariest Alphabet Book.* Austin, TX: Earin Press, 2002.

Ernst, Lisa Campbell. *Stella Louella's Runaway Book.* New York: Simon & Schuster Books for Young Readers, 1998.

Fleming, Denise. *The First Day of Winter.* New York: Henry Holt, 2005.

Floca, Brian. *The Racecar Alphabet.* New York: Atheneum Books for Young Readers, 2003.

Ford, Bernette. *First Snow.* New York: Holiday House, 2005.

Fraser, Mary Ann. *I.Q. Goes to the Library.* New York: Walker & Company, 2003.

George, Lindsay Barrett. *In the Garden: Who's Been Here?* New York: Greenwillow Books, 2006.

George, Lindsay Barrett. *The Secret.* New York: Greenwillow Books, 2005.

Gerstein, Mordicai. *The Man Who Walked Between the Towers.* Brookfield, CT: Roaring Brook Press, 2003.

Giovanni, Nikki. *Rosa.* New York: Henry Holt, 2005.

Gorbachev, Valeri. *The Big Trip.* New York: Philomel, 2004.

Harris, Trudy. *100 Days of School.* Brookfield, CT: Millbrook Press, 1999.

Haugen, Brenda. *The 100th Day of School.* Minneapolis, MN: Picture Window Books, 2004.

Henkes, Kevin. *Kitten's First Full Moon.* New York: HarperCollins, 2004.

Herman, Charlotte. *The Memory Cupboard.* Morton Grove, IL: Whitman, 2003.

Hines, Gary. *Thanksgiving in the White House.* New York: Henry Holt, 2003.

Hoban, Tana. *Count and See.* New York: Simon & Schuster Books for Young Readers, 1972.

Hobbs, Leigh. *Old Tom's Holiday.* Atlanta, GA: Peachtree, 2004.

Hodgson, Mona. *Bedtime in the Southwest.* Flagstaff, AZ: Rising Moon, 2004.

Holiday, Billie, and Arthur Hernog Jr. *God Bless the Child.* New York: HarperCollins, 2003.

Hopkinson, Deborah. *A Packet of Seeds*. New York: Greenwillow Books, 2004.

Hopkinson, Deborah. *Under the Quilt of Night*. New York: Atheneum Books for Young Readers, 2001.

Juster, Norton. *The Hello, Goodbye Window*. New York: Hyperion Books for Children, 2005.

Keller, Holly. *Farfallina & Marcel*. New York: Greenwillow Books, 2002.

Kelly, John, and Cathy Tincknell. *The Mystery of Eatum Hall*. Cambridge, MA: Candlewick Press, 2004.

Kimmelman, Leslie. *Round the Turkey: A Grateful Thanksgiving*. Morton Grove, IL: Whitman, 2002.

Kirk, David. *Dashing through the Snow*. New York: Callaway, 2005.

Kottke, Jan. *A Day with a Librarian*. New York: Children's Press, 2000.

Kroll, Virginia. *Really Rabbits*. Watertown, MA: Charlesbridge, 2006.

Krull, Kathleen. *The Boy on Fairfield Street*. New York: Random House, 2004.

Lehn, Barbara. *What Is a Teacher?* Millbrook, CT: Millbrook Press, 2000.

Lester, Helen. *Tacky and the Winter Games*. Boston: Houghton Mifflin, 2005.

Leuck, Laura. *Jeepers Creepers: A Monstrous ABC*. San Francisco, CA: Chronicle Books, 2003.

Leuck, Laura. *One Witch*. New York: Walker & Company, 2005.

Martin, Jacqueline Briggs. *Snowflake Bentley*. Boston: Houghton Mifflin, 1998.

Mayr, Diane. *Littlebat's Halloween Story*. Morton Grove, IL: Whitman, 2001.

McKissack, Patricia C. *Messy Bessey's Holidays*. New York: Scholastic, 2001.

Medearis, Angela Shelf. *Seven Spools of Thread*. New York: Scholastic, 2005.

Milgrim, David. *Thank You, Thanksgiving*. New York: Clarion Books, 2003.

Mora, Pat. *Tomas and the Library Lady*. New York: Alfred A. Knopf, 1997.

Morris, Ann. *That's Our Librarian!* Brookfield, CT: Millbrook Press, 2003.

Murphy, Mary. *Koala and the Flower*. Brookfield, CT: Roaringbrook Press, 2001.

Nagda, Ann Whitehead, and Cindy Bickel. *Polar Bear Math*. New York: Henry Holt, 2004.

Numeroff, Laura. *If You Give a Pig a Party*. New York: Laura Geringer Books, 2005.

Old, Wendie. *The Groundhog Day Book of Facts and Fun*. Morton Grove, IL: Whitman, 2004.

O'Malley, Kevin. *Straight to the Pole*. New York: Walker & Company, 2003.

Pallotta, Jerry. *The Beetle Alphabet Book*. Watertown, MA: Charlesbridge, 2004.

Pallotta, Jerry, and Ralph Masiello. *The Skull Alphabet Book*. Watertown, MA: Charlesbridge, 2002.

Parish, Herman. *Amelia Bedelia, Bookworm*. New York: Greenwillow Books, 2003.

Park, W.B. *Who's Sick!* Boston: Houghton Mifflin, 1983.

Pattison, Darcy. *The Journey of Oliver K. Woodman*. New York: Harcourt, 2003.

Polacco, Patricia. *Christmas Tapestry.* New York: Philomel Books, 2002.

Polacco, Patricia. *An Orange for Frankie.* New York: Philomel Books, 2004.

Rey, Margaret, and H.A. Rey. *Curious George Visits the Library.* Boston: Houghton Mifflin, 2003.

Richardson, Adele D. *Transport Helicopters.* Mankato, MN: Bridgestone Books, 2001.

Robbins, Ken. *Seeds.* New York: Atheneum Books for Young Readers, 2005.

Rose, Deborah Lee. *The Twelve Days of Kindergarten.* New York: Abrams, 2003.

Ross, Michael Elsohn. *Snug as a Bug.* San Francisco, CA: Chronicle Books, 2004.

Ross, Tony. *Centipede's 100 Shoes.* New York: Henry Holt, 2003.

Rylant, Cynthia. *All I See.* New York: Orchard Books, 1988.

Rylant, Cynthia. *If You'll Be My Valentine.* New York: Harper Collins, 2005.

Samuels, Barbara. *Happy Valentine's Day, Dolores.* New York: Melanie Kroupa Books, 2006.

Schertle, Alice. *All You Need for a Snowman.* New York: Harcourt, 2002.

Schnur, Steven. *Autumn: An Alphabet Acrostic.* New York: Clarion Books, 1997.

Schulman, Janet. *10 Trick-or-Treaters: A Halloween Counting Book.* New York: Alfred A. Knopf, 2005.

Shange, Ntozake. *Ellington Was Not a Street.* New York: Simon & Schuster Books for Young Readers, 2004.

Sierra, Judy. *Wild about Books.* New York: Alfred A. Knopf, 2004.

Slate, Joseph. *Miss Bindergarten Plans a Circus with Kindergarten.* New York: Dutton Children's Books, 2002.

Slate, Joseph. *Miss Bindergarten Takes a Field Trip with Kindergarten.* New York: Dutton Children's Books, 2001.

Spinelli, Eileen. *In Our Backyard Garden.* New York: Simon & Schuster Books for Young Readers, 2004.

Spinelli, Eileen. *The Perfect Thanksgiving.* New York: Henry Holt, 2003.

Spinelli, Eileen. *Something to Tell the Grandcows.* Grand Rapids, MI: Eerdmans Books for Young Readers, 2004.

Spohn, Kate. *Turtle and Snake's Valentine's Day.* New York: Viking, 2003.

Stanley, Diane. *The Giant and the Beanstalk.* New York: HarperCollins, 2004.

Stanley, Diane. *Goldie and the Three Bears.* New York: HarperCollins, 2003.

Thaler, Mike. *The Librarian from the Black Lagoon.* New York: Scholastic, 1997.

Thompson, Carol. *Mr. Wiggle Looks for Answers.* Columbus, OH: Waterbird Books, 2004.

Thompson, Carol. *Mr. Wiggle Loves to Read.* Columbus, OH: Waterbird Books, 2004.

Thompson, Carol. *Mr. Wiggle's Library.* Columbus, OH: Waterbird Books, 2004.

Ultimate Digital-Stereo Library Sound Effects, The. Universal City, California: Empire Musicwerks, Inc., 2005.

Vestergaard, Hope. *Hello, Snow!* New York: Melanie Kroupa Books, 2004.

Wallace, Nancy Elizabeth. *The Valentine Express.* New York: Marshall Cavendish, 2004.

Wells, Rosemary. *Emily's First 100 Days of School.* New York: Scholastic, 2000.

Wheeler, Lisa. *Hokey Pokey: Another Prickly Love Story.* New York: Little, Brown and Company, 2006.

Wheeler, Lisa. *Sailor Moo Cow at Sea.* New York: Atheneum Books for Young Readers, 2002.

Wilder, Laura Ingalls. *Farmer Boy.* New York: HarperTrophy, 1933.

Williams, Judith A. *Why Is It Snowing?* Berkeley Heights, NJ: Enslow, 2005.

Williams, Suzanne. *Library Lil.* New York: Dial Books for Young Readers, 1997.

Wilson, Karma. *Animal Strike at the Zoo It's True!* New York: HarperCollins, 2006.

Wilson, Karma. *Bear Stays Up for Christmas.* New York: Margaret K. McElderry Books, 2004.

Wilson, Karma. *A Frog in the Bog.* New York: Margaret K. McElderry Books, 2003.

Winne, Joanne. *A Day with a Mechanic.* New York: Children's Press, 2001.

Winthrop, Elizabeth. *Dancing Granny.* Tarrytown, NY: Marshall Cavendish, 2003.

Wood, Audrey. *Alphabet Mystery.* New York: Blue Sky, 2003.

Wood, Don, and Audrey Wood. *Merry Christmas, Big Hungry Bear!* New York: Blue Sky Press, 2002.

Woods, Mae. *Dr. Seuss.* Edina, MN: Abdo, 2000.

Woodson, Jacqueline. *Coming On Home.* New York: G.P. Putnam, 2004.

Yates, Philip. *Ten Little Mummies.* New York: Viking, 2003.

Ziefert, Harriet. *I Wish Santa Would Come by Helicopter.* New York: Sterling, 2004.

Web Site Resources

www.hachettebookgroupusa.com/authors/65/857

www.desertusa.com/animal.html

www.nationalzoo.si.edu

www.whatsthatbug.com

www.mapquest.com

www.delta.com

www.amtrak.com

www.greyhound.com

www.yahooligans.com

www.awesomelibrary.org/

www.enchantedlearning.com/subjects/butterfly/

www.thetravelbug.net

www.tooter4kids.com/Spiders/Spiders.htm

www.kidtravels.com

http://pathways.thinkport.org

www.ala.org//ala/emiert/corettascottkingbookawards/corettascott.htm

Index

About the Authors

Patricia A. Messner has been an elementary media specialist for the past eighteen years in the Lebanon City School District, Lebanon, Ohio. She earned her Masters of Education degree from Miami University, Oxford, Ohio, and her Bachelors in Elementary Education at Asbury College, Wilmore, Kentucky.

Brenda S. Copeland has been an elementary librarian for the past ten years in Palmyra School District, Palmyra, Pennsylvania. She earned her Masters of Library Science degree from Kutztown University and her Bachelors in Elementary Education at the University of Delaware.

Brenda and Pat are a sister team up who grew up in Southwestern Ohio. They have completed this book over the phone and the Internet. Every Sunday afternoon the world comes to a standstill as Brenda and Pat talk over the week's events and plan the next step, whether it is a section in their book or a story that needs some sparkle. Ideas and lessons are reworked and added to as the sisters share their library skills. Lesson plans are traded by e-mail and practiced in their library and media center classrooms, both in Ohio and Pennsylvania, several times before they appear on the desk of Sharon Coatney, Libraries Unlimited Editor.

This dynamic pair love to dress alike and appear at conferences and book signings. They dream of one day getting their children's stories published.

Other books written by these authors are *Linking Picture Books to Standards* (Libraries Unlimited, 2003), *Collaborative Library Lessons for the Primary Grades* (Libraries Unlimited, 2004), and *Using Picture Books to Teach Language Arts Standards in Grades 3–5* (Libraries Unlimited, 2006).